8 July, 2019

For Kate

SAMUEL BECKETT
THE MIDDLE AND LATER YEARS

If you ever find 'THE EARLY',
let me know.

David

SAMUEL BECKETT

The Middle and Later Years

DAVID CAMERON

Greenwich Exchange
London

Greenwich Exchange, London

First published in Great Britain in 2019
All rights reserved

Samuel Beckett: The Middle and Later Years
© David Cameron, 2019

Printed and bound by imprintdigital.com
Cover design by December Publications
Tel: 07951511275

Greenwich Exchange Website: www.greenex.co.uk

Cataloguing in Publication Data is available
from the British Library

ISBN: 978-1-910996-29-4

In memory of Michael Degning

CONTENTS

CHRONOLOGY

1906
Samuel Barclay Beckett born on 13 April (Good Friday) in family home at Foxrock, a suburb of Dublin. Father a quantity surveyor, mother formerly a nurse. One older brother, Frank.

1920-1923
Attends Oscar Wilde's old school, Portora Royal School, County Fermanagh, Ireland (Northern Ireland, following partition in 1921).

1923-1927
Studies Modern Languages (French and Italian) at Trinity College Dublin (TCD); at college, plays first-class cricket.

1929
First publication, a critical essay in defence of James Joyce; ends brief relationship with Joyce's daughter, Lucia, who becomes increasingly mentally ill.

1930
Prize-winning poem 'Whoroscope' published; lectures unhappily at TCD; meets painter Jack B. Yeats, whose work impresses and influences him.

1931
Critical study of Marcel Proust published.

1932
Resigns from TCD; finishes novel *Dream of Fair to Middling Women*, published after his death.

1933
Father and cousin, Peggy Sinclair, die; begins psychoanalysis in London with influential analyst Wilfred Bion.

1934
Collection of stories *More Pricks Than Kicks* published.

1935
Attends lectures by leading psychoanalyst C.G. Jung; poetry collection *Echo's Bones and Other Precipitates* published.

1938
Stabbed in Paris by a pimp; begins relationship with future wife, Suzanne Déscheveaux-Dumesnil; novel *Murphy* published.

1940	Joins French Resistance cell.
1942	Forced to flee with Suzanne to Roussillon (Vaucluse), where he writes novel *Watt*.
1945	On visit to Ireland, has moment of vision which shapes future literary career; works for Irish Red Cross at Saint-Lô, Normandy; awarded Croix de Guerre for his Resistance work.
1946	Begins writing fiction in French, including *Mercier et Camier*.
1947-1949	Writes work for which he is most remembered – trilogy of French novels and play *Waiting for Godot* (En attendant Godot).
1950	Mother dies, after gradual decline due to Parkinson's Disease.
1952	Has house built near village of Ussy-sur-Marne, a place for writing and refuge.
1954	Brother Frank dies.
1955-1958	Plays *Endgame* (Fin de Partie), *All That Fall* (for radio) and *Krapp's Last Tape* written and performed.
1960	Begins play *Happy Days*.
1961	Novel *Comment C'est* published, three years before English version, *How It Is*; continues affair with Barbara Bray but marries Suzanne.
1962-1963	Writes *Play*.
1965	Writes *Eh, Joe* (for television); *Film* starring Buster Keaton released.
1969	Awarded Nobel Prize for Literature.
1972	Writes play *Not I*.
1976	Directs Billie Whitelaw in a production of play *Footfalls*.

PROLOGUE

SAMUEL BECKETT IS SO REVERED A writer that one website dedicated to the avant-garde (ubu.com) carries a photograph of him glowering over the contents of its homepage, with no accompanying quote or caption, just the square-cut grey hair, wrinkled skin, and steely gaze visible through dark glasses. He is the watchful master, overseeing proceedings like the bespectacled eyes of Doctor T.J. Eckleburg on the billboard overlooking the Valley of Ashes: which is a metaphor, from *The Great Gatsby*, for atheistic Western Man's vision of God – second only in fame, perhaps, to Beckett's own, forever-absent Godot.

In an early 1990s sitcom, the late Irish comedian, Sean Hughes, would face tricky situations by musing 'What would Beckett do?' He was speaking for a whole generation of the intelligent, sensitive young for whom Beckett was an uncompromising master artist. 'The truth about Beckett,' wrote Robert Nye, 'is that he stands in danger of becoming the patron saint of writers.' Beckett's death conferred not sainthood but godhead.

The Nobel Prize in Literature had been awarded to Beckett in

1969, two months after the Northern Ireland riots which heralded the start of 'the Troubles' (the presentation speech spoke of 'a country divided'). The Academy wasn't going to let down Ireland again, having neglected to award the prize to James Joyce. Beckett had been close to Joyce in Paris, had read to him, been loved by Joyce's adored but highly disturbed daughter Lucia, and even taken dictation when Joyce was composing his punning opus, *Finnegans Wake* (famously, there had been a knock at the door during one such dictation; Joyce said 'Come in' and Beckett included the words, which Joyce let stand).

The similarities and differences between these two great Irish writers are worth considering. Both were modernist pioneers, both were Irish (county Dubliners), and both lived as exiles. But modernism's claim on Beckett is less certain than its claim on Joyce: was Beckett really (as one of his biographers asserts) the 'last modernist' – or the epitome of postmodernism (that recently fashionable movement of self-referentiality)? They were different sorts of Irishman, too: Joyce a Catholic who endured increasing levels of poverty in his childhood and sympathised with the Irish nationalist cause (while rejecting its 'old pap of racial hatred'); Beckett from a respectably middle-class, Anglo-Irish Protestant background, residing at a boarding school in the north when the Partition of Ireland occurred, and adept at the 'West Brit' sport of cricket while at Trinity College Dublin.

In literary terms, what do these differences of upbringing matter? Joyce's writing is 'catholic' in the sense of all-embracing, while Beckett is temperamentally drawn to bareness and barrenness: *Finnegans Wake* grew out of a sketch called 'Here Comes Everybody'; Beckett's motto could be 'Nobody Comes Here'. But Beckett put it best himself when he contrasted his approach with Joyce's, writing to his official biographer: 'My own way was in impoverishment, in lack of knowledge and in taking away, in subtracting rather than adding.' While both writers continue to be revered, it is Beckett who seems like our contemporary still.

These pages cover the Middle and Late Beckett, and also Beckett the poet, for poetry was the wellspring of Beckett's maturity. Nobody interested in Beckett would want to be without an early work as entertaining as the novel *Murphy*, with its opening sentence – 'The sun shone, having no alternative, on the nothing new' – as good as any he wrote. But though some readers prefer the early prose work for its caustic humour and wordplay, others reject it as immature and even (as in the satirical portrait of Beckett's first love – and first cousin – Peggy Sinclair) misogynistic. While everything in his maturity exists in the early work in embryonic form (and whose work doesn't?), there are few authors whose writing so demonstrably shows a new beginning – effectively a clean break. Beckett (who claimed to be able to remember being in the womb) was, as a writer, born again.

There was a lot of living, and suffering, to be got through before that. He was the younger of two sons born to Bill and May Beckett: the couple met when Bill was a patient in the hospital where May worked as a nurse – Bill was still reeling from his relationship with a Catholic woman being abruptly ended by her parents' disapproval. A family friend asserted that 'Bill never got over it, never.' May was practical and efficient but, like her younger son, prone to bouts of depression – he said of himself as a child that he had 'little talent for happiness'. Being sent away to boarding school might adversely affect any sensitive child, but, if anything, Beckett's level of unhappiness grew less.

An outstanding Modern Languages student at Trinity College Dublin, at age 22 he went to the École Normale Supérieure in Paris as *lecteur d'anglais*. It was through his friendship with the poet Thomas MacGreevy that he came to know Joyce in Paris. But he was required to return to Trinity to teach there, which he loathed, and he resigned his lectureship. After both his beloved father Bill and Peggy Sinclair died, he moved to London for psychoanalytic treatment at the Tavistock clinic. In 1936, he witnessed the barbarity of the Nazis at first hand on a trip through Germany. A year later he returned to Paris after falling out with his mother; he was already the published author of a story collection, and soon *Murphy* was accepted for publication.

Beckett's apparently motiveless stabbing by a pimp on a Paris street led to him being hospitalised and visited out of sympathy by an acquaintance, Suzanne Déscheveaux-Dumesnil, who became his companion and later his wife. Beckett joined a Resistance cell in occupied Paris during the War but was betrayed by a priest who was in reality an agent of the Nazis. Beckett fled with Suzanne to south-eastern France, where he wrote the novel *Watt*. In 1945, he returned to Paris and also took the opportunity to visit his mother and his brother, Frank, in Ireland. He was taken aback by his mother's frailty, but the two got on much better than before. And it was in her bedroom on this visit that he experienced a pivotal revelation which transformed his writing. Soon he was composing the major works that brought him fame for the rest of his life.

'It's the extreme that's important,' Beckett once said. And if you suppose that a modernist experimenter *would* say that, here is what Thomas Hardy, an innovator within traditional forms and a writer as pessimistic and unsettling as Beckett, had to say on the subject:

> I prefer late Wagner, as I prefer late Turner, to early (which I suppose is all wrong in taste), the idiosyncrasies of each master being more strongly shown in these strains. When a man not contented with the

grounds of his success goes on and on, and tries to achieve the impossible, then he gets profoundly interesting to me. Today it was early Wagner for the most part: fine music, but not so particularly his – no spectacle of the inside of a brain at work like the inside of a hive.

The inside of a brain at work like the inside of a hive: one would be hard pressed to come up with a better description than this of Samuel Beckett's writing.

1

THE FIRST AND LAST

Poems

B ECKETT SURPASSED JOYCE AS A PLAYWRIGHT –
Beckett's dismissive comment on the unnecessary in drama,
'The rest is Ibsen', fairly describes Joyce's one play, *Exiles*, but then
Ibsen had been a hero to Joyce – and one can argue that he at least
equalled Joyce's achievement as a writer of fiction (how inadequate
a word!): but, in comparison with their 'major' work, the poems of
both men may be considered slight. Yet for those who rate poetry
above all other literary endeavour, real poems are never 'slight'.

Poetry is the key to understanding both these writers, and not
only because it is inconceivable that the major work of either could
have been written by a non-poet. Joyce and Beckett took their
bearings from poetry. Stephen Daedalus, the hero of Joyce's spiritual
autobiography, *Portrait of the Artist as a Young Man*, is a poet.
Although Stephen persisted into *Ulysses*, Joyce had become less
enamoured of him by then, as of his own youthful self. The thin,
troubadour style of the best of Joyce's poems – notably the one
beginning 'Lean out of the window,/Goldenhair' from *Chamber
Music* – still hold an appeal.

In contrast, Beckett's early poems convey forcefully a young artist's superior contempt. They are written in a style unimaginable in English before the 20th century; unimaginable before 1922, the year of T.S. Eliot's *The Waste Land.*

Any resemblance to Eliot's poem is not coincidental, nor can it be explained by personal affinity. Beckett once walked out of a public lecture being given by Eliot, and privately he called him a 'jewel thief' (not such an insult for Eliot, who famously remarked that 'immature poets imitate; mature poets steal'). But Beckett shared Eliot's awareness that such 19th-century poets as Laforgue and Baudelaire pointed a way for English poetry to go. In the longish poem 'Whoroscope' (1930), Beckett even tacked on a section of notes explaining the more abstruse allusions, exactly as Eliot had done in *The Waste Land.* Both poems choose free verse over traditional poetic form (though Eliot uses regular rhythm and rhyme when deep feeling compels him to); they progress by association rather than logic, with abrupt shifts in style and tone; they utilise religious imagery (St Augustine gets a mention in their notes); they employ a slangy street style of language when it suits; and both attempt to strike a transcendent note at the end, Beckett's 'starless inscrutable hour' beating Eliot's Buddhistic 'Shantih shantih shantih' in the poetic stakes.

'Whoroscope' was written quickly so that it could be entered for a competition. It won Beckett ten pounds and was published as a book. The speed of its composition may even have helped to make it rhythmically alive and memorable in its individual lines. But it is, essentially, a piece of nothing: the regurgitated cud of Beckett's recent reading of a biography of Descartes. If it is inadmissible as evidence of poetic genius, it nonetheless reveals immense linguistic skill, ready to be deployed when a genuine poetic impulse arrived.

The modernism of T.S. Eliot and Ezra Pound rubbed off on

Beckett and is the dominating influence on show in his first collection, *Echo's Bones*. Indeed, the collection's full title includes the words *and Other Precipitates*, just as the title of Eliot's first (and arguably best) collection, *Prufrock*, is lengthened by the self-consciously ironic *and Other Observations*. The amount of undigested private material in *Echo's Bones* would have dismayed Eliot, however. If Beckett had permitted such private material to do its work – to move the reader – then all would have been well. Instead he uses words viciously, keeping the reader at a distance.

Even in the longer poems, this unlovely modernism cannot fully neutralise the occasionally affecting passages. 'Malacoda', written after his father's funeral, reads like a cold exercise in poetry's new style, except for the line 'hear she may see she need not' (repeated with variations) which records, presumably, his mother's descent into grief.

Dublin provides the poems' backdrop, Beckett recording his baleful impressions of city life with relish, just as Eliot had done in *The Waste Land*. Except that London is invested with powerful symbolism in Eliot's poem: as the capital of a dying Empire, it represents the decay of Western civilisation that had been so shockingly apparent in the recent Great War; Eliot's disillusionment – that of a brilliant young American who had thrown in his lot with England and Europe – has tragic *gravitas*. Beckett's disillusionment reads like the disgust of a young man who has hung around the familiar streets of his hometown too long.

More interesting is 'Enueg II', which introduces the two-beat line that forms the basic rhythm of many passages in the novels, stories and plays:

sweating like Judas
tired of dying

tired of policemen
feet in marmalade
perspiring profusely
heart in marmalade
smoke more fruit
the old heart the old heart

– lines which owe nothing to Eliot or Pound, and which would not look out of place in a collection by the Beat poet Jack Kerouac. The first and last poems of *Echo's Bones*, both very short, also anticipate a later development in English poetry: the toughness, at times brutality, of the kind of writing spearheaded in the 1950s and 1960s by Ted Hughes and Thom Gunn. This is 'The Vulture':

dragging his hunger through the sky
of my skull shell of sky and earth

stooping to the prone who must
soon take up their life and walk

mocked by a tissue that may not serve
till hunger earth and sky be offal

Energetic, mimetic language, portraying a natural creature (one of nature's nastiest) that is connected somehow to the bleak wilderness of the poet's own skull and operates godlike in some nightmare vision of the Creation: pure Hughes, in fact. All the same, it is not easy to say what the poem means. There is not a simplistic point being made, as there often is in Hughes's early animal poems. The same is true of the poem which gives the collection its title:

asylum under my tread all this day
their muffled revels as the flesh falls
breaking without fear or favour wind

the gantelope of sense and nonsense run
taken by the maggots for what they are

Familiar Beckett elements are here: obsessive walking as a relief from (but also indicator of) excessive anxiety; 'low' bodily functions (breaking wind); thought continuing unstoppably, approaching meaning, then obscuring it; and the final triumph of decay and death.

The influence of Ezra Pound – particularly the Pound of the early *Cantos* and the 'Chinese' Pound of *Cathay* – can be felt in some of the more successful Beckett poems from the 1930s. There is a warmth unusual for Beckett in the lines from 'Cascando':

the hours after you are gone are so leaden
they will always start dragging too soon

– which is like the warmth Pound managed to get into his translations of early Chinese poetry. Even the cadences are similar. Take the magnificent Pound translation of a poem by Rihaku (Li Po), 'The River-Merchant's Wife: A Letter', which contains the lines:

You dragged your feet when you went out.
By the gate now, the moss is grown, the different mosses,
Too deep to clear them away!

Perhaps it is mere coincidence, but the affecting rhythm of that last line is reproduced in the line from 'Enueg II', 'too late to darken the sky', which is given emphasis by (near) repetition towards the poem's end.

There are other, more obvious elements reminiscent of the Pound whom Eliot described as 'the inventor of Chinese poetry for our time'; lines such as 'grave suave singing silk' and 'rain on the bamboos flower of smoke alley of willows'.

This evocation of the mystical East alongside images of 'Guinness's barges' and 'the Portobello Private Nursing Home' – like the different poetic influences on display, not only Pound and Eliot, but Dante, Goethe, the Provencal poets, and others – makes *Echo's Bones* an odd fish indeed. Only the difficult four lines that constitute the collection's best poem, 'Da Tagte Es', belong with the similarly brief work of the poet's maturity. Biography tells us that the poem was composed in memory of his late father, but even without this knowledge a sensitive reader of poetry could tell that the rather cryptic lines (Beckett's poems are like codes, the critic Martin Esslin said) resulted from an event that carried deep feeling for their author:

> redeem the surrogate goodbyes
> the sheet astream in your hand
> who have no more for the land
> and the glass unmisted above your eyes

Beckett may have been thinking of those 'surrogate goodbyes' of his as he left on his journeys abroad, particularly the one following his resignation from Trinity College, about which he continued to feel guilty (at having let his parents down) even into old age: in this painful context, 'redeem' is not too strong a word.

'Da Tagte Es' – rhythmically tight and rhyming *abba* (coincidentally appropriate for a poem about a father), but 'difficult' – transcends modernist v traditionalist polemics. In many curious respects it resembles a short poem it predates, 'Nuns and Fish' by Robert Graves, a writer very different in temperament from Beckett:

> Circling the circlings of their fish,
> Nuns walk in white and pray;
> For he is chaste as they,
> Who was dark-faced and hot in Sylvia's day,
> And in his pool drowns each unspoken wish.

There are similarities of diction in the last two lines, as well as a closed-in-on-itself feeling achieved partly by the rhyme. In a rare meeting with Graves, T.S. Eliot said of this poem: 'That's certainly real poetry, the real thing! But what does it mean, and how on earth did you do it?' Both poems are 'the real thing' and read like the involuntary expression of intense emotion crystallised into dense and difficult language.

Beckett was unusual as a poet in that he was able to write real poems (in Eliot's sense of the word) that were not in his mother tongue. French brought a new simplicity and purity to his poems, though the two English poems 'Cascando' and 'Saint-Lô' indicate that he was already on his way, just as the English novel *Watt* displays some of the maturity of the French prose. Beckett's own translations of his French poems contain such memorable lines as:

> the summer rain rains on my life
> on me my life harrying fleeing

Occasionally, the translation may even surpass the original. This is Beckett's translation of the last of Quatre Poèmes:

> I would like my love to die
> and the rain to be falling on the graveyard
> and on me walking the streets
> mourning the first and last to love me

In later editions of Beckett's poems, the last line becomes the more literal translation of 'pleurant celle qui crut m'aimer': 'mourning her who thought she loved me'. This destroys what, in English, is a touching and effective poem, though one verging on sentimentality, it is true. In the more literal translation, Beckett is displaying a novelist's (not a poet's) superior knowledge: '*I* know what she felt, even if *she* didn't'. There may be self-deception in saying 'the first and last to love me' – after all, how can he know? –

but it is a self-deception appropriate to the feeling of self-pity. And a poem of self-pity should at least be self-pitying.

Beckett rejected the Celtic Twilight strain of poetry that was in the ascendant in Ireland when he was a young man, preferring to put his own psyche under the microscope rather than draw romantically on a national 'myth kitty' (Philip Larkin's phrase). In doing so, he exploited many of the strategies of modernism, notably the use of irony to ensure a proper distance.

Why is it that so major and so poetic a writer turned out not to be a major poet? Well, it simply doesn't follow that major + poet = major poet: poetry may be said to 'fly by all the nets'. There is a mono-mood in Beckett, akin to the tension of endless, unrelieved waiting such as Beckett explored in *Waiting for Godot*.

Thomas De Quincey relates how he and his friend William Wordsworth were on a walk while anxiously waiting to read news of the Peninsular War: Wordsworth, having put his ear to the ground to hear what he thought was the approach of the mail carrier bringing the London newspapers, rose disappointed and spoke about the senses' heightened state of sensitivity in the moment of relaxation after a period of tension. It seems that poetry and poets require flux, a tension of opposites which finds at least temporary resolution at the moment of insight – which may be one reason why poetic genius is routinely associated with manic depression. Beckett had all of the necessary poetic equipment, which he deployed superbly throughout his plays and fiction, but the troughs vastly outnumbered and outplumbed the peaks.

It is likely that very few would have heard of Beckett if he had written nothing but poetry, but this misses the point – which is that Beckett was, as his long-time publisher John Calder described him, 'a poet in everything he wrote'.

2

BANISHMENT

First Love; The Expelled; The Calmative; The End

WRITTEN JUST AFTER THE WAR, THE minor prose works *First Love* (Premier amour), *The Expelled* (L'expulsé), *The Calmative* (Le calmant) and *The End* (La fin) marked a major turning point for Beckett. These were his first works of fiction in French, a language which freed him from the too-literary Irishness, in part imitative of Joyce, which characterised his early writing. Beckett said privately about the English language that 'you couldn't help writing poetry in it'. He probably meant by this that he was easily seduced into writing 'poetically' in the worst sense, producing the kind of prose which is in fact the polar opposite of poetry. One of Beckett's greatest achievements is that, in the late work especially, he did indeed manage to write a recognisably 'poetic prose' in English that had the hallmarks of true poetry.

It was in French that he began to strip language bare. Still experiencing a compulsion to write, he no longer felt compelled to do so in his mother tongue: an act of separation equivalent to his escape from suburban Foxrock and a loving, but stifling, mother. The sub-Joycean acrobatics of the early novels and stories persisted into his next work in French, *Mercier et Camier*. Nevertheless, it is with these first short French texts (translated into English by Beckett, *The Expelled* and *The End* with Richard Seaver's assistance) that a line is drawn in the sand, indicating where the real Beckettian desert begins.

With slight variations, and whether expelled by others or not (a leave-taking symbolic of birth – a botched birth), the characters in these stories begin a journey that takes them through various unsatisfying locations, where they have apparently meaningless encounters with other people, until they are alone in increasingly smaller womblike surroundings – caves, cabs, boats – fantasising about finding peace or extinction in the sun (son). As for the locations, the word 'grandeur' is used not wholly ironically in this description of a mountain cabin from *The End*: 'The scene was the familiar one of grandeur and desolation.' Beckett's childhood wanderings with his father over the coastal hills of Dublin's outskirts provide much of the detail of the external world in these stories. 'But there was never any city but one ... I only know the city of my childhood,' says the narrator of *The Calmative*, and any doubt about its Irishness is dispelled by the Hiberno-English question that follows: 'Was I hungry itself?' Country, town and city are wandered into and out of, but nowhere satisfies. Ultimately, the locations are all internal, the product of tormented inner life: 'we are', says the narrator of *The Calmative*, 'needless to say in a skull'.

These stories are not allegories but they partake of the allegorical. Beckett probably had Dante in mind – he often had – when he settled on this form of the quasi-allegorical, episodic journey for much of his major and minor work in prose. The narrator of *The Calmative* says that he will tell his story 'as though it were a myth, or an old fable'. The people met along the way are like those souls encountered by Dante in the *Inferno* and *Purgatorio* (there is no paradise in Beckett). In later work, the Beckett narrator often feels that he is 'accompanied by a shade' on his journeys. The shade is his father, as Dante's guiding shade for much of his journey was Virgil. The bald, brown-suited comedian and his audience encountered in *The Calmative*, for instance, seem fixed in this situation and these identities forever: there is no before or after. The description of the scene reads like a prose translation of a verse from *The Divine Comedy*:

> Their shrill laughter pierced the clapping and, when this had subsided, broke out still here and there in sudden peals even after the next story had begun, so that part of it was lost.

The sudden and unsubtle use of a non-naturalistic style in *The End* – 'One day I had met a man I had known in former times. He lived in a cave by the sea ... ' – diminishes the story's power. Despite those aspects of his style which would in time feature in the postmodernist's bag of tricks, Beckett knew how to sustain illusion. But he had not mastered this yet. Even when he had, the illusion created was far from conventional, and the difficulty that many readers have with Beckett's writing is its apparent lack of either progression or tension.

The Expelled begins with an expulsion. The narrator has been thrown out of some undefined religious and charitable institution and told never to come back. Thus, we are in a world where charity is its opposite, and where, by implication, faith and hope are similarly absent. By making the expeller a religious charity, Beckett offers an ironic rebuke to Christianity. 'They were most correct, according to their god,' the narrator of *The Expelled* says.

In *Down and Out in Paris and London*, George Orwell observed that for some hopeless, decent people, going to a Salvation Army shelter was 'their last clutch at respectability'. Similarly, Beckett's tramps often reveal themselves (at least by implication) to be, like Beckett, respectably middle class in origin. Orwell threw himself into poverty before writing about the life of the down-and-out, but Beckett had no political or sociological mission in writing about society's dispossessed. He did not really write 'about' them at all. There are details in these characterisations which seem psychologically accurate, but that is incidental and reflects Beckett's own sense that he was apart from, not a part of, socially adjusted humanity. Cunning is present in the Beckett tramp, as it needs to be in anyone living on the street. The narrator of *The End* calculates the best means of collecting money: not in a tin at his feet, he observes, since 'people who give alms don't much care to toss them, there's something contemptuous about this gesture which is repugnant to sensitive natures'. Another example of Beckett's thinking in character in these stories is his tramps' exposure to – at times, their posing of – a sexual threat. The motives of anyone befriending them are often suspect. The narrator of *The Calmative* wakes up on a stone seat to find a man sitting beside him, a befriender who indulges in sexual talk before offering a phial (presumably of 'calmative', ie sedative) in exchange for a kiss. 'I knew there were kisses in the air,' the narrator says.

There is more to Beckett's misfits than cunning: 'sour and mistrustful', they are aware of their inadequacy, at times more so than others ('He was delighted to see me, poor man'). The pathos of their own situation is not lost on them. There is a gentle irony, worthy of Jane Austen, in a statement such as 'Fortunately I did not need affection'. *First Love* is bright with the frostiness of such deliberately unsentimental irony – the dominant state of mind of Beckett's narrators. The punning and witty graveyard humour of the opening pages is reminiscent of the gravedigger's scene in *Hamlet*. In Shakespeare, this kind of humour is referred to as 'comic relief': a device for preventing emotional exhaustion in the audience. Worth considering is its purpose in relation to the *writer's* emotions. This is the expression of a mind almost overwhelmed by powerful feelings, attempting to find relief in light-hearted and perverse wordplay. (The comedy of a depressive such as Spike Milligan comes into this category.) Beckett, strongly affected by his father's death in 1933 (the pain of which was not eased by his mother's insistence on a prolonged Victorian-style period of mourning), deals with this subject almost callously in *First Love*. In this instance, the callousness is a disguise. Words are used to keep genuine emotion at bay, but its presence can be inferred.

Beckett's down-and-outs prefer to be without hope, since hope would demand some kind of exertion from them. Occasionally we see them reflected in other people's eyes. The narrator of *The End* is told that he is neither as old nor as sick as he thinks. (Beckett, even when relatively young, seemed to need to imagine himself as old and sick; in this respect, he resembled another leading modernist, T.S. Eliot). They remember what it was like to have been a child, to receive affection and to have it withheld from them. The warmth of the father-son relationship recalled in *The End* is allowed to survive Beckett's usual ironic undercutting: 'I would have liked him to draw me close with a gesture of protective love, but his mind was on other things.' Just when we think we have the measure of a Beckett character, a sudden shift can take place. Thus, in *The End*, the down-and-out narrator mentions in passing his 'tutor' – an expert on ethics, apparently – and his son, an 'insufferable son of a bitch', glimpsed (uncertainly) on the street.

Somewhat disturbing is the attitude to children revealed or implied in these stories. In *The Calmative*, there is an erotic element to the description of an encounter with a young boy ('the pretty curve of the long bare legs all muscle and dirt'). Occasionally, as in some of Kafka's work, the mere presence of children is felt to be threatening: staple scene of many horror films, a small child will appear and look on silently and sinisterly. The narrator of *The End* is visited in his basement hovel by a red-headed girl:

> She lingered awhile in the room, then went away without a word. One day I had a visit from a policeman. He said I had to be watched, without explaining why.

The attitude to children in *The Expelled* is straightforwardly sadistic, uncomfortably so. In describing his loathing, the narrator sounds comically like the Child Catcher in *Chitty Chitty Bang Bang*:

> ... these nasty little creatures, their prams, hoops, sweets, scooters, skates, grandpas, grandmas, nannies, balloons and balls, all their foul little happiness in a word ...

Beckett, liberated by his use of the first-person narrative, is able to think and say the preposterous worst. Or not quite the worst, since even in this example the narrator only *fantasises* about lynching children and babies: he is 'not a violent man', although one who would gladly 'encourage the others and stand them drinks when it was done'. This is funny, of course. In this vein of humour, the breaking of taboos is followed by a reflex of laughter. Perhaps the reason Beckett holds back from an excess of cruelty in the stories – apart from his characters being too passive to indulge in anything so active – is that his work is much more visibly an expression of his own troubles and neuroses than the work of more conventional authors, or even of those modernist and postmodernist authors who contrive to be absent from their 'texts'. The narrators of these stories do not quite become characters with whom a reader can or cannot identify: despite the many and repetitious references to the body and its ailments in a Beckett work, the narrator feels more like a disembodied consciousness than a physically alive human being. *The Expelled* partly fails in this respect: repelled by the cruelty, we distance ourselves from the narrator who becomes therefore more of a 'character' about whom – as about anyone we meet in daily life – we can form an opinion. This was not a problem without a solution, however, and Beckett went on to explore the psychology of deliberately inflicted cruelty more effectively in his plays, where characters really could exist and emotional distancing formed part of his technique.

As radical a departure as the new writing signalled in terms of style, one continuity with the early work is Beckett's use of undercutting irony and bathos: the expansive, pretentiously lyrical is undercut by the banal, vulgar and plain. The result is, in the words of his biographer Anthony Cronin, a kind of 'joke style'. This undercutting technique is deployed for humorous effect – and without humour, Beckett's work would hardly be readable – but is also consistent with the inconsistency of the narrator's point of view and the philosophical impossibility of stating truth. A typical example from *The Calmative* – 'They were the perishing oaks immortalised by d'Aubigné. It was only a grove' – is not lingered over but occurs in mid-flow, and cumulatively these examples of undercutting do not fragment the text but define one characteristic of the narrator's mind: we get used to them much as we get used to (while still noticing) a person's stammer. In the later work, this style becomes much more than a joke. We can see signs of this already. The grove in *The Calmative* is described further:

> Yes, no matter where you stood, in this little wood, and were it in the furthest recess of its poor secrecies, you saw on every hand the gleam of this pale light, promise of God knows what fatuous eternity. Die without too much pain, a little, that's worth your while.

The angry corrective to the lyrical – the command 'Die without too much pain ... ' – is a recurring feature of Beckett's writing, and seems to indicate an exasperation with the ease with which words can tempt the mind to deviate in its search for truth, or from the attempt to say something which is at least not untrue.

One can be too analytical in commenting on Beckett's humour: sometimes he just tells jokes. In *First Love*, the narrator observes that 'women smell a rigid phallus ten miles away and wonder, How on earth did he spot me from there?' The influence of comedians from the silent film era and the early talkies on the physical comedy of Beckett's plays is well known: it is also possible to hear the voice of Groucho Marx delivering such jokey lines as these (also from *First Love*):

> I have two rooms, she said. Just how many rooms do you have? I said. She said she had two rooms and a kitchen. The premises were expanding steadily, given time she would remember a bathroom.

The description later in the story of the woman undressing underlines the fact that Beckett – had he possessed a more conventional, less despairing mind – might have been a straightforwardly comic writer.

In each of the stories, the narrator's hat, shoes, and clothes figure prominently. Most people come to Beckett through seeing or reading *Waiting for Godot*, and they are struck immediately by this circus clown or vaudeville fooling with hats and boots and so on. A greatcoat is one of Beckett's favourite garments for his characters – and perhaps one of his favourite words too. 'Give me back my greatcoat,' the discharged narrator says in the first page of *The End*. A symbol of the self – or, more accurately, the self that would exist if only coherence could be achieved – the greatcoat functions as a security blanket, thus taking the character back to his babyhood, and also as an inheritance from the father, so propelling him towards a manhood that is never attained. *The Calmative* is explicit about this:

> I was wearing my long green greatcoat with the velvet collar, such as motorists wore about 1900, my father's, but that day it was sleeveless, a vast cloak. But on me it was still the same great dead weight, with no warmth to it ...

In *The Expelled*, the hat is also connected with the father. The narrator recalls his father marching him to the hatter as soon as he is old enough. 'I have often wondered,' he says, 'if my father's purpose was not to humiliate me.' Which is how adult initiation appears to its 'victim' – a child who, after all, continues to exist inside the initiated adult self. Ill-fitting clothes in Beckett's work, as well as simply indicating unease about being in the world, convey symbolically this feeling of inadequacy in assuming the 'mantle' of one's father and one's ancestors generally: the clothes are too tight, just as the norms handed down by our predecessors are too restrictive.

John Keats wrote in a letter to his brothers that 'a Man of Achievement, especially in Literature' was 'capable of being in uncertainties, mysteries, doubts, without any irritable reaching after fact and reason'. Beckett's revelation in his mother's bedroom was that he had been stupid to hide his uncertainty and ignorance, and he decided that these negative qualities would become the mainspring of his writing. The typical Beckett character – nothing if not irritable, and a man of *un*achievement – exists in a permanent state of uncertainty ('Negative Capability', Keats called it) that cannot be resolved in terms of final philosophical or theological statements, not even the assertion Nietzsche put into the mouth of his Zarathustra, that 'God is dead'. The lack of certainty becomes a quality of the prose too: a contrast with the all-knowing, all-seeing third-person narration of his early novels and stories. *The Expelled*, for example, begins with an attempt to be precise about the number of steps the narrator has fallen down, but his indecisiveness about where such a count properly begins and ends means that the narrative is not permitted even this slight degree of certainty.

Beckett, perhaps *too* uncertain how plausible this new kind of story should be, occasionally has his narrators explain what they are up to. In *The Expelled*, it is remembering in order to avoid being overcome by memory. 'Memories are killing,' the narrator says. This is very far from the Proustian view that the truth of life is somehow secreted in involuntary memory. In *The Calmative*, the narrator is telling himself stories in order to ease his anxiety, just as his father had soothed him by reading a bedtime story about a 'Joe Breem, or Breen, the son of a lighthouse-keeper, a strong muscular lad of fifteen, those were the words, who swam for miles in the night, a knife between his teeth, after a shark, I forget why, out of sheer heroism' (more a stirring than a soothing story, but the comfort would have come from repetition and the father's presence). The stories he now tells himself are of defeat not heroism.

The religious, looking for religious meaning in Beckett's books, find it. Beckett hardly encouraged them in what little he had to say about his work, but he did strew his writing with biblical references. Like a good Protestant, in his later years he made sure that the sparsely-furnished rooms he wrote in contained a Bible – the prose of the King James Version was part of his mind's furniture. He was no believer, but he was unable to commit himself positively to unbelief either. These early stories are riddled with references to Christianity. Although other writers who were not committed Christians have felt free to exploit Christian symbolism in their work, Beckett's use of it is disturbingly different. In *Dr Zhivago*, the Russian poet-novelist Boris Pasternak described contemporary reality while expressing a tragic sense of life that drew on allusions to the Gospels. This approach is too high-minded for Beckett, who toys with the tragic. The effect is strangely, and appropriately, empty.

The narrator of *The End* goes one better than Mary and Joseph by being refused lodging in a stable (a stable with a manger features in the final page of *The Expelled* also), and one better than Christ on his triumphal entry into Jerusalem by being jeered at as he travels on an ass. His degradation is more complete than theirs. Begging, he partly assumes the posture of the crucified: 'Now and then to rest my neck I dropped my head on my chest.' A political street orator, who points to him as evidence of social iniquity but cannot bear his unresponsiveness, cries out: 'Can you hear me, you crucified bastard?' 'My hour was not yet come,' he says at one point. Nor does it come. It is as though a cunning tramp were living a pantomime version of Christ's Passion. The image of Christ on the cross is conjured up in *The Expelled*, the narrator disapproving of the undisciplined way in which people make the sign of the cross when a funeral cortege passes. In *The Calmative*, bats are referred to as 'flying crucifixions'. One of the locations in this story is a cathedral that seems emptier of God (and less haunted by His absence) than the 'accoutred frowsty barn' of Philip Larkin's piously agnostic poem 'Churchgoing'.

A curious mixture of dependence and independence, the narrators of these four stories – like so many of Beckett's characters – would prefer to be left in a room and have food brought to them and have their chamber pot emptied occasionally; but once driven to leave the room and fend for themselves, sooner or later they shun all human contact. Only the narrator of *First Love* manages to fall (comically) in love, and even to live with a woman for a while, though the man-woman relationship quickly degenerates to a foetus-mother one. Sexual love is too threatening, since sexual excitement undermines the already shaky stability of the self. 'What goes by the name of love is banishment,' the narrator says, 'with now and then a postcard from the homeland.' Home – mother, father, childhood, the womb – is the self's bedrock. (Not irrelevantly, Beckett was born in the Foxrock family home.) The narrator, once he finds himself tracing his beloved's name in a cowpat, knows for sure that his love is not merely Platonic. Eventually he has his 'night of love': so he infers, waking up and seeing his woman naked beside him. When she gets pregnant – by him, she says, though if she is, as she claims, a prostitute, the father might be one of her clients – he tries to console her with the thought that it was 'just wind'. The sustained comedy makes the extraordinary passage that follows unexpected. At the level of realism, it is simply that she draws back the curtain to show him her swollen belly while he looks out at the scenery instead. However, the scenery described – that of the coastal landscape Beckett had explored with his father – is similar to the 'visions' of the narrator of *The End*, once he is secure at last in the womb-substitute of a boat he has sealed himself into:

> She had drawn back the curtain for a clear view of all her rotundities. I saw the mountain, impassable, cavernous, secret, where from morning to night I'd hear nothing but the wind, the curlews, the clink-like distant silver of the stone-cutters' hammers. I'd come out in the daytime to the heather and gorse, all warmth and scent, and watch at night the distant city lights, if I chose, and the other lights, the lighthouses and lightships my father had named for me, when I was small, and whose names I could find again, in my memory, if I chose, that I knew.

The landscape is in effect seen *inside* the woman's pregnant belly, and not to left or right of it: a merging of father and mother (male and female) associations which takes us back to the story's magnificent opening sentence: 'I associate, rightly or wrongly, my marriage with the death of my father, in time.' Beckett affects to eschew this sort of coherence in his writing: at the end of *The Expelled*, for example, the narrator wonders why he had bothered to tell this story, since he could just as easily have told another one. In fact, he could not. The range of Beckett's subject matter is incredibly narrow, suggesting that choice played little part in it. Coherent, funny, and profound, *First Love* is a jewel in Beckett's oeuvre, a worthy forerunner of the three great prose works he was soon to write.

3

OBSERVING THE MOON

Waiting for Godot

O N THE RUE GODOT LE MAUROY one day, a prostitute
with whom Beckett did not want business asked who he was
waiting for – Godot? Of the many stories and theories put forward
to explain the title of one of the half dozen most important plays of
the 20th century, this anecdote of Beckett's is at least not the most
boring.

Waiting for Godot (En attendant Godot) was begun towards
the end of 1948 and took Beckett less than four months to write. It
saved his sanity, he said. He was in the middle of the most productive
period of his writing life, and had just completed the first two novels
of the so-called Trilogy. *Godot* provided a temporary relief from
the fatiguing solipsism of the longer novelistic work. The evidence
of pleasure – even joy – in the play's writing is everywhere evident.
'Energy is eternal delight,' William Blake wrote, and this play of
despair, boredom and impotence is both energetic and delightful.

Two clownish tramps wait at a country road for a Mr Godot to
keep his appointment with them. They encounter only the self-
proclaimed owner of the land accompanied by a 'menial' whom he

abuses, and the messenger boy come to announce once again that Godot is sure to be there tomorrow. Meanwhile they must repeat or devise distractions in order to kill time and give themselves the impression that they exist. The most adverse criticism that any audience might direct at the play is put into the mouth of one of the characters: 'Nothing happens, nobody comes, nobody goes, it's awful!' It only seems that way. Things do happen, and characters come and go, their natures changing in the course of the play.

The two leading characters, Vladimir and Estragon, behave in many respects like an old married couple, 'blathering about nothing in particular ... for half a century', their different but complementary natures creating friction and also dependence. When Estragon says of the Holy Land: 'That's where we'll go, I used to say, that's where we'll go for our honeymoon. We'll swim. We'll be happy,' one's first reaction is to think of 'we' as referring to himself and Vladimir, rather than a youthful relationship with some woman. (Similarly, the British comic duo Morecambe and Wise – a later incarnation of the Laurel-and-Hardy type which influenced Beckett – used to appear in their television shows in bed together: a strangely unsurprising version of the married couple.) Although the same sentiment and gesture appear to be merely automatic elsewhere, there is pathos in Estragon's wondering at the end of the first act if they wouldn't have been 'better off alone' since they 'weren't made for the same road', and their embrace at seeing one another again at the start of the sombre second act appears genuine. Vladimir recognises that he is the more protective of the two, mothering Estragon to some extent ('There ... there ... Didi is there ... don't be afraid ... '). It is possible to find an element of hope in the persistence of this friendship. ('Hell is other people' is the sentiment of one of Sartre's plays, not this one.) It is equally possible to find such a reading sentimental.

Despite their atrocious memories, both Vladimir and Estragon have glimpses of a shared past, 'the good old days' in which they were freer, possibly dandyish, picking grapes in the red-soiled 'Macon country'. When Vladimir says that they should have thought of losing heart 'a million years ago, in the nineties', one might think of the Decadents of the 1890s (Ernest Dowson, Lionel Johnson, Arthur Symons, Oscar Wilde, etc). In certain respects, Vladimir and Estragon represent the ignoble fate of the artist-as-outsider. Beckett had endured many years on the sidelines, waiting for recognition. Had he gone on writing more novels in the *Murphy* vein, his achievement would have been real but minor: a kind of kicking against the pricks of Victorian literature and sensibility without ever leading to the discovery of his distinctive voice.

The characterisation of Vladimir and Estragon continues the Cartesian mind-body duality expressed in *Murphy* and elsewhere in Beckett. Vladimir is the highly-strung thinker, whereas Estragon is the earthy poet-type (he gestures towards his rags as evidence that he was once a poet). Vladimir is often more eloquent, in that style used again and again by Beckett – pretentiously high-minded to begin with, but ending flatly – whereas plainness marks the speech of the more taciturn Estragon. The view of the poet embodied by Estragon is decidedly unsentimental: less a superior being or symbol of transcendence (though he has his moments) than an oafish lump wrapped up in his own physical and material concerns. Estragon cannot even be described charitably as a poet of the earth in the Wordsworthian sense: he dismisses Vladimir's concern with place, exclaiming: 'You and your landscapes! Tell me about the worms!'

This attitude towards poetry in the play, however ironic, resembles that of the Greco-Armenian mystic G.I. Gurdjieff, whose view of man's mechanicalness did not make an exception of poetry. That the poet is dead too is one of the play's uncomfortable truths.

And yet *Waiting for Godot* is a supremely poetic text. It locates and delineates certain states of mind and being in a way that feels intuitively right, and could not have been predicted logically from its source material (such as Beckett's experiences during the Second World War, much of it tedious, waiting for messages to arrive from other Resistance members or simply for the war to end). It has the internal logic of a dream. When Godot's messenger boy exits running near the end of the first act, what arrives is not Godot but night (in both acts, the moon rises once Godot's non-appearance is certain), an event which Estragon marks by misquoting lines from Shelley's poem 'To the Moon'. The waiting is over for one more day:

> [... *The light fails. In a moment it is night. The moon rises at back, mounts in the sky, stands still, shedding a pale light on the scene.*]
> VLADIMIR: At last! [ESTRAGON *gets up and goes towards* VLADIMIR, *a boot in each hand. He puts them down at the edge of stage, straightens and contemplates the moon.*] What are you doing?
> ESTRAGON: Pale for weariness.
> VLADIMIR: Eh?
> ESTRAGON: Of climbing heaven and gazing on the likes of us.

This is Shelley's poem in full:

I

And, like a dying lady lean and pale,
Who totters forth, wrapp'd in a gauzy veil,
Out of her chamber, led by the insane
And feeble wanderings of her fading brain,
The moon arose up in the murky east,
A white and shapeless mass.

II

Art thou pale for weariness
Of climbing heaven and gazing on the earth,
    Wandering companionless
Among the stars that have a different birth,
And ever changing, like a joyless eye
That finds no object worth its constancy?

That unforgettable image of the dying lady in her 'gauzy veil',
and the reference to the 'feeble wanderings of her fading brain',
make one think of such later dramatic works of Beckett's as *Not I*
and *Footfalls*. According to his biographer James Knowlson, on
coming across Caspar David Friedrich's painting *Man and Woman
Observing the Moon* in a Berlin gallery (there is a similar painting
by Friedrich, *Two Men Observing the Moon*), 'Beckett announced
unequivocally: "This is the source of *Waiting for Godot*, you know."'
The narrator of *Malone Dies* also refers to the Romantic German
painter, the moon, and waiting: 'It is such a night as Caspar David
Friedrich loved, tempestuous and bright ... If I had the patience to
wait I would see the moon.'

If one is on the lookout for meaning in *Godot*, there are so many
possible leads within the text itself that it might seem odd to
emphasise the importance of what is not there: Woman. More
specifically, Woman as Moon Goddess, the source of poetic
inspiration. In comparison with the perception of the Goddess's
presence, man's attempts at creating meaning are mere instances
of ratiocination. 'Watch ye therefore: for ye know not when the
master of the house cometh': but Godot cannot come at just any
hour of the day or night – night is not his realm. Salvation – not a
commodity bestowed by the Goddess – is possible only during the
day, when there is a chance that Godot will arrive. Not even human
company is permitted during the night. When they meet up again

in the morning, the comparatively rational Vladimir cannot bear to hear Estragon recount his dreams. Estragon is a poor sort of poet by day, but unlike Vladimir he always manages to be beaten up in the night. By his visions, perhaps?

Beckett's extensive reading in philosophy and his absorption of scripture inevitably find their way into this drama which flirts with ultimate questions of life's meaning, ridiculing the answers offered by philosophy and religion. 'The end,' said Beckett, 'is to give artistic expression to something hitherto almost ignored – the irrational state of unknowingness where we exist.'

Christ and God certainly exist in the play insofar as they are spoken of by the characters, none of whom mentions that the first syllable of 'Godot' is 'God'. Vladimir exclaims, 'Christ have mercy on us!' when he learns from the messenger boy that Godot has a white beard. They are waiting for Godot in order to be saved, yet he resembles a childish view of a wrathful, jealous Old Testament God (God + OT?). Inverting the Cain and Abel story, in which it is the shepherd brother who is the favoured one, Godot beats the messenger boy who tends the sheep, sparing his brother. Vladimir explains that Godot would punish them if they ever stopped waiting and left the place.

If at one time there was a tendency to overplay the importance of religion in *Godot*, the reverse is now true. But it is worth considering that a dramatic work of existential despair written now would be unlikely to contain so many biblical allusions. In this play, Beckett was reflecting his Irish Protestant upbringing.

If at a climactic moment in a work by Albert Camus a character exclaimed, 'We are men!', we would be entitled to think of this as a positive assertion of humanity in the face of the absurd. But in *Godot*, Vladimir says this when all four main characters are on the ground unable to get up. Ironically, Pozzo had been calling for help for some time, and now that Vladimir and Estragon have also fallen over, Vladimir can say: 'We've arrived'. The inference is that only divine intervention, not human assistance, could be of any help to humanity. But in Beckett the divine never does intervene.

Above all, perhaps, *Godot* suggests that we do not properly exist; that we are stranded here on earth, waiting for real life to begin. That Beckett experienced this feeling to an unusual degree could potentially have made his work merely subjective in an idiosyncratic way. It is the sort of existential unease which has come to seem characteristic of 'modern man'. *Godot* does not insist that we act authentically in the face of apparent absurdity, though it makes plain that some forms of self-deception are more complete than others. Beckett's work offers as little hope or consolation as Kafka's does. Of the existentialist literature of his time, Camus's *The Outsider* and Sartre's *Nausea* seem closest in spirit: appropriately, since these books do not so much expound a philosophy as express a personal vision.

Other readings are possible, of course. A straightforwardly political meaning is often ascribed to the Pozzo-Lucky (bourgeois-proletarian) relationship. Pozzo's attitude veers between viciously exploitative and pretentiously patrician. The latter is comically apparent when he reflects on his treatment of Vladimir and Estragon:

> I have given them bones, I have talked to them about this and that, I have explained the twilight, admittedly. But is it enough, that's what tortures me, is it enough?

As commentators have pointed out, Beckett had recently had good reason to fear inhuman treatment at others' hands, since his Resistance work might easily have led to his incarceration and death in a Nazi camp, a fate that befell his friend Alfred Perón.

Indignation at human cruelty is even poked fun at, when Vladimir, who has impressively sustained his disapproval of Pozzo's behaviour for several minutes, instantly switches sides once Pozzo appears to break down over 'the way he [ie Lucky] goes on'. Vladimir recovers his distaste for Pozzo, resorting to violence against him in the second act. He is certainly more preoccupied than Estragon by the way Pozzo treats Lucky, perhaps sensing in his weaker moments a possible model for lording it over Estragon. He occasionally apes Pozzo's manner of uttering single word commands, and suggests to Estragon that they 'play at Pozzo and Lucky'. If there is a point to be made here, it is perhaps that even when justifiably indignant we can allow the thing we protest against to make too deep an impression on our souls. It begins to intrigue us.

Waiting for Godot, a play that reflects Beckett's post-War situation and the state of mind he most often found himself in, connects with a post-religious malaise that afflicted western man in the 20th century, a malaise that began before then and has continued since. But even this is not enough to explain the resonance that *Godot* still has for many theatre-goers and readers. As a spectacle, this innovative modernist drama presents the audience with comfortingly familiar elements of popular entertainment – shades of vaudeville, the circus, music hall, early cinema – and treats a subject universally familiar: the experience of waiting, that state of mind in which tension, anxiety, boredom, hope and dread compete for dominance. Waiting partly obliterates the present moment, while making it loom larger in consciousness as time drags. In this context, everyone can identify with a feeling of unease within the present. Existential malaise is difficult to portray in fiction and drama – the protagonist of Sartre's *Nausea*, for example, is made to see the meaninglessness and contingency of life by an almost mystical revelation, an event which paradoxically gives his life meaning – but Beckett is able to reach more than just an artist-outsider audience by using so commonly experienced a situation, even if it is taken to absurd extremes.

The waiting game in *Godot* appears at times to be profoundly significant, religiously so; at other times it is on the everyday palliative level of Scarlett O'Hara's final words in *Gone With the Wind*, 'After all, tomorrow is another day.' As Vladimir says, 'The essential doesn't change.' Our atrophying Reason and distracting senses keep us from the despair of Pozzo, now blind and without his solid bourgeois perception of clock-time, who says:

> One day, is that not enough for you, one day like any other day, one day he went dumb, one day I went blind, one day we'll go deaf, one day we were born, one day we shall die, the same day, the same second, is that not enough for you? [*Calmer.*] They give birth astride of a grave, the light gleams an instant, then it's night once more.

There are several highly quotable, apparently 'key' passages in the play – comparable with, say, Hamlet's 'To be or not to be' or Macbeth's 'Tomorrow and tomorrow and tomorrow' speech – around which an interpretation of the play's 'message' might be built. But this rhythmically convincing passage does seem more significant than most. Nor is it limited to the psychology of one character in a particular situation, as even Hamlet's and Macbeth's words are, since Vladimir soon takes up and extends the metaphor in the same impersonal voice:

> Astride of a grave and a difficult birth. Down in the hole, lingeringly, the gravedigger puts on the forceps. We have time to grow old. The air is full of our cries.

Contrastingly, Pozzo's earlier 'lyrical' passages, such as the one beginning 'The tears of the world are a constant quantity', are comic parodies of the profound. They have the cadences and diction of sermons, political rhetoric, prophecy of the Kahlil Gibran sort – language which, when one stops hearing it as meaningful, sounds merely vacuous, humorously so. Oliver Sacks put on record the reaction of aphasia sufferers to a televised speech by the then US President, Ronald Reagan: they burst out laughing. The audience at a performance of *Waiting for Godot* is similarly privileged – if one may put it this way – and sees the comedy which the characters generally miss. This laughter is directed at characters whose deteriorated faculties are worsening. Vladimir, the play's custodian of Reason, reckons that at one time he and Estragon must have been capable of thought: how else, he asks, could one account for 'these corpses' ('These skeletons,' Estragon adds): the ragged remnants of thought surviving in their habit-formed speech. In order to know the substance of such thought, the audience – or, more likely, the reader – would have to work back from the actual words of the characters to piece together a more meaningful exchange – and existence – for the characters (like the 'anti-psychiatrist' R.D. Laing scrutinising the meaning of so-called word salads produced by so-called schizophrenics).

Scholars have certainly attempted this with the most deteriorated speech of all: Lucky's. The gist of Lucky's stream of words (a performance he is forced to give) is roughly that, despite man's supposed progress and the distractions he devises for himself, he continues to 'waste and pine'. The speech is certainly a moment of climax, after which there is a more elegiac, less energetic tone to the play. Its language is at once breathlessly urgent, panted out mainly in short bursts with two stressed syllables ('abode of stones/ in the great deeps/the great cold', etc), and not urgent at all, since it issues from an emotional deadness. At the opposite extreme to this garbled monologue is perhaps the play's most striking linguistic feature, the rapid to-and-fro between Vladimir and Estragon, an 'antiphonal' style that is like one character's dialogue chopped up and divided between two:

> ESTRAGON: And what did he reply?
> VLADIMIR: That he'd see,
> ESTRAGON: That he couldn't promise anything.
> VLADIMIR: That he'd have to think it over.
> ESTRAGON: In the quiet of his home.
> VLADIMIR: Consult his family.
> ESTRAGON: His friends.
> VLADIMIR: His agent.
> ESTRAGON: His correspondents.
> VLADIMIR: His books.
> ESTRAGON: His bank account.
> VLADIMIR: Before taking a decision.

Although *Godot* would seem to mark a complete break with the influence of Joyce on Beckett's writing, it is worth taking a look at Joyce's short story 'Ivy Day in the Committee Room' from *Dubliners* to see a possible (and probably subconscious) source for the play. The story describes the paralysis of early 20th-century Irish politics, as embodied by a group of rather dissolute political canvassers. The exchange between the men and a boy who brings them beer is not unlike the exchanges between Vladimir and Godot's messenger boy. The spirit of the dead, revered (but betrayed) 19th-century Irish nationalist politician, Charles Stewart Parnell, broods over proceedings just as the similarly absent figure of Godot does in Beckett's play.

But it is Lucky's speech which anticipates the style of the later parts of the novel Beckett was soon to write, *The Unnamable*, as well as his most experimental (and arguably least readable) prose work, *How It Is*: a style which he would deploy most successfully in a later dramatic masterpiece, *Not I.*

The English version of *Waiting for Godot* has 'A tragi-comedy in two acts' under the title. Beckett's characters come closest to speaking truth when they are made aware of tragedy; when, the illusion of hope receding, they have least to lose. *Godot* gives us dark truths but also humour and playfulness when the characters attempt to keep these truths at bay. In the years to come, Beckett learned how to write more concisely and ingeniously for the theatre, and at times he even spoke disparagingly of *Godot.* But the world is right to persist in thinking it a great work.

4

THE FRENZY OF UTTERANCE

Molloy; Malone Dies; The Unnamable

IN THE EXTENDED PROSE WRITING OF the three novels known as 'the Trilogy', the now identifiable Beckett character is shown in all his disintegration, and the theme of the regressive journey accorded sufficient space for a full unravelling. There are so many points of comparison between the novellas and the novels that the former read like sketches for the latter. The difference is in the degree of (to use an odd word for Beckett) fulfilment. The writing becomes more completely a world of its own; the reading of it more completely an act of contemplation.

All three novels were written in French in a relatively short space of time (astonishingly short, when one considers the rarity and brevity of his subsequent prose writing): between May 1947 and January 1950. Beckett also spent a few months in this period writing *Waiting for Godot*. Even if the late work succeeded in getting closer to the stark perfection Beckett sought, those three novels and that one play constitute Beckett's 'major' achievement (as such works of sustained brilliance are called), his main claim to fame and to a place in posterity.

Molloy

The structure of *Molloy* makes it recognisably a novel. Molloy's account of his journey to find his mother and 'settle the matter' between them is followed by the account of a man, Jacques Moran, sent on a mission to find Molloy. The language of each part is appropriate to the character of the narrator: Molloy deteriorated, Moran solid and bourgeois – until he goes the same way as Molloy and essentially becomes him. Moran's 'journey from my country to Molloy's' is a journey towards *dis*illusionment, the stripping away of illusion. As a work of fiction, it is a forerunner of the kind of metaphysical detective story written by the American author Paul Auster. With Beckett, however, there is even less of an attempt at plausibility, and no reader could miss the metaphorical dimension of Moran's search.

Above all, perhaps, *Molloy* is a lengthy demonstration of Beckett's discovery of his distinctive voice as a writer, and the conceit of Moran's mission to seek out Molloy allows him to discard this voice temporarily before picking it up again.

In his dead mother's bedroom, Molloy is writing the story he relates. A nameless other – but there may be more than one – keeps him alive, taking away what he has written and returning it marked with signs he doesn't understand: a writer-jailor metaphor which evokes the atmosphere of the War and covert operations for the Resistance. Those who mark Molloy's writing could be the censors of the enemy or of his own side. It is completely indeterminable and so hardly matters – the predicament remains the same in either case. Likewise, Moran is writing his report for someone in a position of power over him, his mysterious employer Youdi, whose instructions are conveyed through a fellow agent, Gaber. But as Moran nears Molloy's deteriorated state, his account becomes less the report of a conscious mind than the documenting of an inner voice: 'And the voice I listen to needs no Gaber to make it heard,' he says, meaning that he needs no intermediary.

Beckett is exploring the predicament of the writer who writes for God – a deity who, in Beckett, enjoys only partial authority. Before he sets out on his journey, Moran – having drunk a lager shortly before receiving Communion – reflects that 'God would know, sooner or later'. This view of the incompleteness of God in Beckett's writing can be viewed as a form of Gnosticism. In Gnosticism, both Creation and Creator are seen as flawed. Unlike the Creator (or Demiurge), the True God is not responsible for matter. There are also intermediate beings – Aeons, in Gnostic philosophy; Gaber and Youdi (among others) in *Molloy* – between this True God and ourselves.

The first few sentences of *Molloy* recall Camus's existentialist novel *The Outsider*, the opening words of which are as famous as any in modern literature: 'Mother died today. Or perhaps yesterday, I can't be sure.' Anthony Cronin describes these sentences by Camus as 'somewhat Beckett-like', but it would be fairer to say that Beckett is here somewhat Camus-like. And not only at the beginning: Moran kills a man he encounters with as much detachment as Camus's protagonist kills an Arab. Molloy's narration begins: 'I am in my mother's room. It's I who live there now.' That second sentence is aggressively boastful (like the words of the Labour attorney general, Sir Hartley Shawcross, after his party's landslide victory in the 1946 General Election: 'We are the masters now'). *Molloy* and *The Outsider* require the immediate death of the mother to set the groundwork for what follows: a callousness that leads inevitably to the later almost-unreal murder in each book.

Molloy echoes Camus's character Meursault when he asks about his mother: 'Was she already dead when I came? Or did she only die later? I mean enough to bury. I don't know.' But the tone of the

narration soon diverges from that of *The Outsider*. Beckett just
about reins in the black comedy but not the mental fragmentation
which makes the sentences as sharp as broken glass. Once we get
to Moran's story, sentences lengthen and ooze their comforting
vowels for a while – not incidentally becoming less quotable, as
though frenzied collapse were a requirement of poetic genius.

For Molloy, the journey to the mother represents the possible
restoration of coherence, an escape from the absurd confusion his
existence has become. Not that he has an overly sentimental view
of his mother, a woman he describes as having 'brought me into
the world, through the hole in her arse if my memory is correct.
First taste of the shit.' It is a matter of indifference to him whether
he calls her 'Ma, Mag, or the Countess Caca'. Nevertheless, he
recognises that everything he feels driven to do is bound up with
this relationship:

> And of myself, all my life, I think I had been going to my mother, with
> the purpose of establishing our relations on a less precarious footing ...
> hoping to do better the next time.

In the light of this passage, it is moving to reflect on the ageing
Beckett's repeated use in one late prose work (*Worstward Ho*) of
the phrase 'fail better'. Just as Joyce claimed never to have left
Ireland, so Beckett can be said to have returned repeatedly to the
family home in Foxrock in his writing.

It is from just such a home that the patriarchal Moran sets out,
his son in tow. Having a son allows Moran to inflict on another the
same sort of misery Youdi inflicts on him. Despite the occasional
lapse into sentimental indulgence, Moran's approach to fatherhood
is essentially sadistic:

> The thought that between my death and his own, ceasing for an instant
> from heaping curses on my memory, he might wonder, in a flash,

whether I had not been right, that was enough for me ...

The shift from sentimentality to sadism can take place within a single sentence. Gregory Bateson's theory of the 'double bind' – an intolerable situation in which, no matter what a child does, he or she cannot win – is worth mentioning here. Metaphysically, the double bind (which Bateson saw as a root cause of schizophrenia) is very relevant to Beckett's writing, since – in Beckett's eyes – no matter what human beings contrive to do, they always lose. The state of being physically bound recurs in the writing. Here, Moran's relationship with his son is a precursor to that between Pozzo and Lucky in *Waiting for Godot*, as is clear from Moran's statement: 'I toyed briefly with the idea of attaching him to me by means of a long rope.' He is not unaware of his own cruelty, acknowledging that 'If I had been my son I would have left me long ago'. He is his own son and he does leave himself, since in Beckett's novels and novellas having a son is the equivalent of being a son. Molloy fantasises that he once had a son, then says more definitely that this son wasn't the offspring of true love ('The true love was in another') – and, of course, Beckett was himself the offspring of a rebound relationship formed after his father's failed love affair had resulted in nervous collapse.

The need for involvement in a father-son relationship does not diminish with age, and the disintegrating Moran longs for Molloy to come and 'be like a father' to him. Anti-bourgeois satire is combined in Beckett with a longing for the comfortably-off conventional father. In the enigmatic story of A and C who pass each other by on an after-dinner walk in the countryside, Molloy imagines each to be 'like so many citizens, dreaming and farting'. This slightly contemptuous attitude does not prevent him from longing to know and feel everything about this other:

> I want to see the dog, see the man, at close quarters, know what smokes, inspect the shoes, find other things.

– precisely what a novelist ought to be able to do. But Beckett is barred (or bars himself) from such intimate knowledge of the other. Indeed, the uncertainty of the narration not only reflects Molloy's mental confusion but also suggests an authorial self-consciousness, a worm of doubt. Beckett could pull the rug from under the reader's feet at any moment, and yet this never quite happens; the fiction does not entirely self-destruct: there is the sense that narrator and author are equally *driven* to an extremity of utterance. The 'joke' in Beckett is not only at the expense of 'literature' – of the traditional novel, for example – but also at the earnest modernist reinvention of literary form to capture all aspects of life and humanity. Humanity just isn't worth the effort:

> The fact is, it seems, that the most you can hope is to be a little less, in the end, the creature you were in the beginning, and the middle.

The form traditionally ascribed to the novel – of having a clear beginning, middle and end – will do for the life of the individual too, as long as it is understood that one progressively becomes *less*.

Just about the only real action in the first part of *Molloy* is humorously reminiscent of that staple episode of the 19th-century novel: the poor unfortunate being taken in by the socially respectable for the purposes of improvement, waking up with clean linen and the possibility of a clean slate. Cycling erratically, Molloy runs over a dog, and is saved from a baying mob by the owner, a Mrs Loy or (Molloy decides on) Lousse. She had loved the pet, she says, like her own child. Now she replaces one substitute-child with another by admitting Molloy to her home. As he says elsewhere: 'Against the charitable gesture there is no defence.' Soon feeling like a prisoner in 'Lousse's house', he discerns a sexual motive behind her charity.

Molloy is essentially a Dantesque journey, spiritual in nature, towards a beatific vision. This is, admittedly, an odd comparison, like equating Botticelli's 'Venus' with Picasso's 'Dora Maar'. Yet what are those artistic depictions if not of 'Woman as Muse' in very different centuries? Mrs Loy/Lousse is the earthbound parody of the Madonna-figure pursued by Molloy and Moran. Challenged by a ruddy farmer with lantern and spade, Moran says that he is on a pilgrimage to the 'Turdy Madonna':

> She is the Madonna of pregnant women, I said, of pregnant married women, and I have vowed to drag myself miserably to her niche, and thank her.

Beckett's mature style functions, at times, like Hamlet's madness, allowing him to speak outrageously, so that we hardly notice the (for Beckett) terrifying thing that is actually being said. Terror is in fact the key emotion in Beckett's writing. Molloy describes himself as 'so terror-stricken that I was virtually bereft of feeling, not to say of consciousness, and drowned in a deep and merciful torpor shot with brief abominable gleams'. This terror is located in the mother: 'my mother' says Molloy, 'whose image ... was beginning now to harrow me again'. A related fear of homosexuality is also part of the terror. Molloy even doubts if Mrs Loy/Lousse, 'a woman of extraordinary flatness', was a woman at all. Thinking back to the sexual relations with his 'one true love', he wonders if 'after all she put me in her rectum ... Perhaps she too was a man.' Beckett, now in his forties, knew very well that he had not escaped the terrifying hold his mother had on him. If Molloy records a journey (or two journeys), it is not clear if this is a journey from or towards the mother. Explicitly, it is a journey *towards*; implicitly, a journey *from*. Molloy imagines an internal desert landscape: 'an Egypt without bounds, without infant, without mother'. In his radically new style of writing, Beckett sought to replicate this Egypt.

Malone Dies

The dying Malone sets out the threefold nature of his narrative intention from the start – 'Present state, three stories, inventory' – and fails to deliver adequately in each part (the inventory of his possessions is only ever talked about, not made). Essentially, *Malone Dies* (Malone meurt) repeats the situation at the beginning of *Molloy*, even using (with slight variations) some of the same words: 'I do not remember how I got here. In an ambulance perhaps, a vehicle of some kind certainly.' Malone's invented character, Macmann ('Son of Man'), ends up in a bewildering confinement similar to his own, drifting out to sea as his creator expires.

A summary of the 'plot' reveals only the distance Beckett was placing between his own approach (following the revelation in his mother's bedroom) and that of the traditional novel. In fact, the plot as such is merely that an old dying man in a room – of a house, hospital, or asylum – is whiling away his last moments writing, describing his condition as best or worst he can, and making up stories of deteriorated characters who may or may not reveal aspects of his own past or present self. There is also the plot of Malone's own stories – or, possibly, single story, with the main character's name changing along the way. And this is where things become truly surreal. The youngster Saposcat (possibly 'human shit', from homo sapiens and scatology) exists in a stifling, conservative home environment, but is also involved with the brutish farming family, the Lamberts. Later, as the adult drifter Macmann, he ends up in a madhouse called the House of St John of God. Macmann has unsatisfactory sexual relations and 'a kind of intimacy' with his 'keeper', Moll, who has a crucified Christ carved on her tooth and earrings representing the two thieves either side of him. She is superseded as 'carer' by the psychotically cruel Lemuel who goes berserk with a hatchet, killing two inmates during an island trip organised by the ineffectually charitable Lady Pedal. Lemuel orders the small group of survivors, which includes Macmann, into a boat and they drift out to sea, where both Macmann and his creator appear to expire, just as the English language expires in the book's closing words:

> or with his pencil or with his stick or
>> or light light I mean
>> never there he will never
>> never anything
>> there
>> any more

Malone's emphasis on 'play' at the novel's start adds a light touch and is a balancing counterweight (in Malone's own mind also) to the earnestness of his introspection. 'People and things ask nothing better than to play, certain animals too ... I shall never do anything any more from now on but play.' This is said as if in defiance of a strict Victorian parent. (One such, the mother of Robert Graves, instilled in her young son the motto: 'Work is really far more interesting than play.')

In Malone's stories of the Saposcats, we get more than a whiff of the stifling atmosphere of Beckett's Foxrock family home: 'It was as though the Saposcats drew the strength to live from the prospect of their impotence.' Mr Saposcat, like Beckett's father, despairs of his son ever managing to command a salary. And the portrait of little Sapo at school resembles the picture of Beckett at a similar age, as described by his classmates and teachers: liked rather than loved, athletic, impertinent. The life of the Lamberts is the pornographic obverse of the conventionally stifled family life. They represent the other side of the Saposcats' coin, the family hearth turned into a 'secret bestial place' (to use Philip Larkin's phrase).

In an allusion to a passage from the Book of Revelation, Malone promises early on that he 'shall be neither hot nor cold any more' but shall instead 'be tepid'. Similarly, he sets out to show only what he must show, to illuminate just a small part of existence with his 'taper' since 'A bright light is not necessary'. Blank neutrality, minimalism: this sounds like the literary creed of a certain sort – Beckett's sort – of modernist. Yet, here again, Malone 'fails': as so often in Beckett, hysteria is never far from the surface. Sapo identifies with the hawk, 'fascinated by such extremes of need, of pride, of patience and solitude'. Malone is only *resolved* to be tepid: in truth, he is extreme. Not till Beckett's later, supremely minimal work did he perfect the neutral tone that brings out all the deadness of dead pan delivery, as extremity is held suspended in numbness.

Anxiety precludes the possibility of analysis, or at least interferes with its workings. 'I must state the facts, without trying to understand, to the end,' says Malone. His stories, he says explicitly, are vain attempts to ward off the sensation of being alive. So must it have been for Beckett too. The link between character and author is more than inferred: Malone looks forward to his own demise, stating: 'Then it will be all over with the Murphys, Merciers, Molloys, Morans and Malones.' And indeed, this supreme creative phase in Beckett's novelistic (or anti-novelistic) career was meant to end with *Malone Dies*. The Trilogy was unplanned. Perhaps inevitably, the continuation was named *The Unnamable*.

Beckett must often have feared that he was going mad while writing with such intensity and living what he wrote; he would also have been sceptical of what he refers to in *Murphy* as the 'pretentious fear of madness'. The writing of *Malone Dies* almost cost Beckett his health. It could have been worse: as his biographer

Deirdre Bair remarks, 'Everyone close to him feared that he might quite literally die when it was finished.' Likewise, Malone, writing to achieve coherence, disintegrates as he writes. If there is really such a thing as existential literature, this is surely it. And yet, unlike other modern writers whose work excavates hidden depths, Beckett does so with a scepticism and uncertainty so profound that comedy is never far away. His despair cannot quite take itself seriously, which is in itself a desperate situation.

The Unnamable

The ending of *Malone Dies* is not wholly satisfying. The disintegration of syntax and absence of punctuation seem unprepared for, appear too rapidly. (The same might be said of the final lines of Eliot's *The Waste Land*.) They are the last words but yet not *the last word*. Beckett had more to say; or, rather, he had to say less.

The narrative voice of *The Unnamable* (L'Innommable) attempts to do away with stories and named characters, but eventually we are introduced to Mahood and (even further down the fictional food chain) Worm. Once again, the characters of previous Beckett fiction – 'my troop of lunatics' – are named in valedictory fashion:

> To tell the truth I believe they are all here, at least from Murphy on, I believe we are all here, but so far I have only seen Malone.

Elsewhere, the voice says: 'There's no getting rid of them without naming them and their contraptions' and 'nothing doing without proper names'. Speechless, wearing a brimless hat, Malone passes a few feet away, like one of the spectral presences inhabiting Dante's hell and purgatory. D.H. Lawrence – a writer at the polar extreme from Beckett – said that an author sheds his sicknesses in his writing. So with Beckett's characters, each sloughed off like a useless skin, a false self. To reveal what? Surely some central core, the essence of self. Beckett even visualises this being, with the Unnamable's self-description:

> I have always been sitting here, at this selfsame spot, my hands on my knees, gazing before me like a great horn-owl in an aviary. The tears stream down my cheeks from my unblinking eyes. What makes me weep so? From time to time. There is nothing saddening here. Perhaps it is liquefied brain.

The voice toys with the idea that it might become the invented character before last: so, by inventing Worm, it will actually become Mahood. But it concedes defeat. Fiction cannot cancel out despair. 'I thought I was right in enlisting these sufferers of my pain. I was wrong. They never suffered my pains.'

This existential predicament of the writer is explored by Portugal's leading 20th-century poet, Fernando Pessoa, who created alternative selves or 'heteronyms' through which to speak in verse. The question of where authentic suffering lies – with whom – and how literature is used to address/evade such suffering is well expressed in Pessoa's poem *Autopsicografia* (here translated by Martin Seymour-Smith):

> Poets pretend
> They pretend so well
> They even pretend
> They suffer what they suffer.
>
> But their readers feel
> Not the pain that pretends
> Nor the pain that is
> But only their own: that's real.
>
> And so upon toy rails
> Circling reason like an art

Runs round the model train
That's known by the name of heart.

At this point, the question of the *reader*'s relationship to Beckett's writing is worth addressing. The critic Al Alvarez, in a sympathetic study of Beckett, remarked that: '*The Unnamable* gets perilously close to being the Unreadable.' Even taking into account the fact that Alvarez's study came out in 1973, when some of Beckett's more difficult texts (in among the more lucid ones) were still to be written, it has to be admitted that the last book of the Trilogy stretches the goodwill of the 'ordinary, even devoted reader' (Alvarez's phrase) to breaking point. Consisting, after a few pages, of a single paragraph that catches the near-insane flux of a mind at the end of its tether, *The Unnamable* is a kind of literary dead-end, like Joyce's punning dream-fiction *Finnegans Wake*. It is no wonder that it took Beckett another ten years before he could bring himself to write another 'novel' – *How It Is*, which was to be his last. Yet for any reader capable of getting pleasure from the skill with which words are set down on the page, a ghost-written airport book is truly 'unreadable'. Open *The Unnamable* at random and you are sure to find fine writing that holds your attention. But the *cumulative* effect of *The Unnamable*'s style is undeniably wearing.

'Style', though, is too insipid a word to describe what is happening in *The Unnamable*. For Alvarez, what 'comes through most strongly' is 'terror' – terror such as is experienced by the 'chronic schizophrenic'. However, this psychiatric label gets us nowhere. Beckett was not a chronic schizophrenic, nor was he attempting to express with realism the inner life of a sufferer of this condition. He also had good reason not to be overly considerate towards his readers, since at this time he had precious few of these and small prospect of acquiring more. (The fame that was just around the corner must have seemed unimaginable.)

'Ninety-nine per cent of people are out of touch with their spirit,' Beckett told Patrick Bowles, his collaborator on the English version of *Molloy*, and: 'It's the extreme that's important. Only at the *extreme* can you get to grips with the real problem.' If Beckett's writing is not a simplistic search for existential authenticity, nor is it a self-protective meandering to avoid the point. He is trying to get to the human essence, which may perhaps reside in extreme states of mind and being, in the kind of utterance made possible when convention has broken down utterly. The speaker in *The Unnamable* says: 'I alone am man and all the rest divine,' which is a rather Gnostic take on William Blake's insight: 'Everything that lives is holy.' The suffering expressed by Beckett is like the mystic's 'dark night of the soul', with the added despair of night being endless and the mystical vision reduced to gleams in the skull.

5

PENNY FARTHING HELL

Drama After Godot

ENDGAME (FIN DE PARTIE) IS A play of the atomic age, presenting a post-Apocalyptic vision of humanity that would have resonated with audiences in the neurotic Cold War context of the late 1950s. It is also a product of private grief.

Started soon after the death from lung cancer of Beckett's beloved elder brother, Frank, the play is as much about waiting as *Godot* was. This time the wait is almost entirely without hope (if a glimmer of hope can be read into the possible appearance of a small boy near the play's end). 'Something is taking its course,' is a phrase that recurs; and this something is the slow extinction of the blind, wheelchair-bound Hamm, of the relationship between Hamm and his 'servant' Clov, and of the human species itself.

The play's stark setting – 'Bare interior. Grey light. Left and right back, high up, two small windows ... ' – has put several commentators in mind of the interior of a human skull. 'Outside of here it's death!' Hamm shouts to Clov. (For a mind-body dualist like Beckett, everything outside of the skull is indeed deathly.) Their great fear seems to be of human life replicating itself – even, somehow, from a flea or crablouse – in the desolate outside world.

James Knowlson's authorised biography of Beckett describes the brotherly care with which Beckett tended the ailing Frank.

> He developed a routine for passing the days: shaving his brother after breakfast and sharing a late morning whiskey with him; helping him dress for lunch or go outside in the early weeks of his illness; then, as his condition worsened, bringing him up his meals and chatting to him as normally as he could.

This tenderness is transmuted into the ugly, servile solicitations of Clov towards his master. After repeatedly being asked by Hamm if it is time for his painkiller yet (the expected answer, 'Not yet', is the reply reserved for Hamm's outburst on God, 'The bastard! He doesn't exist!'), Clov takes pleasure in telling him: 'You'll never get any more painkiller'. Nor, in this play (Beckett's personal favourite), is the pain ameliorated, which partly explains the hostile critical reaction to its first performances.

The vaudeville comedy and the religious allusions are more muted, and the main relationship on stage is of the sadistic sort reserved for the minor characters Pozzo and Lucky in *Godot*. Here, the minor characters are Hamm's aged, 'bottled'-in-dustbins parents, Nagg and Nell. And whereas in *Godot* a boy appeared at the end of each act as a messenger for Godot, in *Endgame* it is, finally, the appearance of a small boy (seen by Clov through a telescope) which is the visionary/delusionary 'other'. It is as if what was only a herald of possible hope now turns out to be itself the only hope (if even that). *Endgame* confounded audiences who thought *Godot* was drama pared down to the absolute minimum. And the paring down continued well after *Endgame*, in a process which, expressed philosophically, suggests that whatever loss life inflicts, there is always more to lose.

Frank Beckett's terminal illness is not what the play is *about*, but it is one of the play's primary sources. This could explain why, typically for Beckett, the sadistic element is shot through with tenderness: Beckett could never be really nasty in the way that Harold Pinter or Joe Orton, two playwrights he influenced, so obviously could. When Nagg relishes the prospect of his son desperately needing him, this sadistic impulse is described movingly:

Yes, I hope I'll live till then, to hear you calling me like when you were a tiny boy, and were frightened, in the dark, and I was your only hope.

The nastiness is also relieved by characteristically mordant humour:

HAMM: Why don't you kill me?
CLOV: I don't know the combination of the larder.

The image of the boy is taken up again by Hamm in a clear reference to himself – and, one intuits, to Beckett also – in a simile which goes a long way towards explaining the imaginative source of Beckett's fiction and drama:

Then babble, babble, words, like the solitary child who turns himself into children, two, three, so as to be together, and whisper together, in the dark.

But whether the source for the character of Hamm is Frank Beckett or, as some have suggested, Beckett's aunt, Cissie Sinclair (of whom he was fond), or even the near-blind James Joyce with whom Beckett had a master-amanuensis relationship, the important fact is that, for this bleakest of his plays (better than *Godot*, Beckett thought, because 'nastier'), Beckett drew on relationships that were affectionate and therefore meaningful. Even the 'prop' of Hamm's stuffed dog has its origins in the well-loved small dogs that livened up the Foxrock family home. (Curiously, *Godot*'s second act begins with Vladimir singing a roundelay about a dog; though whether this is another religious allusion – 'dog' = backward 'god' – is a question strictly for the birds.)

With its wheelchair-bound, lame, bin-bottled characters, *Endgame* subverts the norm of theatre as dramatic spectacle. Perhaps at this still early stage of his career as a playwright, Beckett felt the need to justify the stilted movement of his drama using dramatic devices. Hence, the theme of chess that is so explicit in the title and Hamm's first (and repeated) words: 'Me to play'. Like cricket, chess was one of Beckett's few enthusiasms, but its use as a structural and thematic device here is arguably unsuccessful. It may have assisted Beckett in the writing of the play (writers need props too), but it adds little, if anything, to the play's undoubted force, and might usefully have been dropped in the final draft. When, in the late 1960s, an actor in a German production asked Beckett's advice on the character of Hamm, he was told that Hamm was 'a king in this chess game lost from the start' and also, confusingly, 'a bad player' – an odd confusion for so sure-footed a writer.

All That Fall was Beckett's first attempt at a radio play and marked a return (though not a permanent return) to writing in English. It is an entertaining work (for those who 'get' Beckett's humour), one that exists for most on the page, as its proper production remains always at the mercy of broadcasters.

While later work would be pared down to the point of evisceration, this piece tells a story and its characters have personality. It is set in rural Ireland, dying rural Ireland, and – like Molloy – has a flavour of murder mystery to it. (It is interesting that Beckett should feel the need to add such a plot hook when exploring new territory or a new medium.) Old Mrs Rooney goes to meet her husband off his usual train, which is unexpectedly delayed; when they do meet up, Mr Rooney speaks about thoughts he had of killing a child; a boy catches up with them to return 'a kind of ball' dropped by Mr Rooney, and reveals the cause of the train's delay: 'It was a little child fell out of the carriage, Ma'am.'

Like *Endgame, Krapp's Last Tape* has had an enduring appeal for theatre producers and audiences. It is one of Beckett's best-loved plays, perhaps because it is about a sort of failure endemic to being alive at all as a human being – the failure to live up to one's youthful hopes for oneself. Regret for love lost – or, more precisely, love discarded – is a poignant aspect of this failure. 'There is no escape from yesterday because yesterday has deformed us, or been deformed by us,' wrote Beckett in his early study of Marcel Proust. And so *Krapp* proves.

The 'action' is set in the future, a point that could easily be missed by an audience today unaware that tape recording technology was fairly cutting-edge in the 1950s (Beckett had seen it at work in a BBC studio in January 1958, as he listened to a recording of *All That Fall*).

An old man, Krapp, searches through reels of tapes on which his younger self has recorded reflections on the year just past and his hopes for the future. On this, his sixty-ninth birthday, he records one more tape – his last. Presumably, Krapp's allotted span on earth will not quite make the biblical lifespan of threescore years and ten. The tape he listens to was recorded thirty years earlier, and in this tape he also comments witheringly on a tape made ten years before that. So we are able to gauge Krapp's decline over four decades. He is a writer whose work has failed to make an impact on the world – unlike Beckett's, though Beckett endured enough years of neglect to know what that was like. 'Good to be back in my den, in my old rags,' his younger self confides to the tape, and there is a sense that Krapp is the sort of writer who gives up on experience to write about it safely in comfort. (But perhaps all writers are like this, to some extent.) Krapp at one time had a revelatory experience which radically altered his approach to writing, as did Beckett. The older, less illusioned Krapp has no interest in listening again to his earlier, effusive account of this revelation (that the inner darkness he had tried to suppress was in fact his greatest strength as a writer), and fast-forwards the tape.

For a weary, 'wearish' old man, Krapp has retained a few pleasures in life: he is still a drinker, disappearing backstage to take regular tipples, and relishes eating bananas ('fatal for a man in my condition' – severe constipation, presumably). He also takes a writer's pleasure in the sound of certain words, such as 'spool' and 'vidua bird'. If there is a duality at work here, it is less between body and spirit (spiritual revelation being rejected) than between body in its present disintegration and body in its past subjection to the pull of lust.

Krapp, recognisably the same man across the years, is forever snooty about his younger self, and continually wrong about the future. His younger self says that he will never sing – and yet the old Krapp sings snatches of the children's hymn 'Now the Day is Over'. (The hymn's second verse – not sung by Krapp – provided the title for a collection of poems bristling with life, D.H. Lawrence's *Birds, Beasts and Flowers*.) The old Krapp is mystified by a reference to a black ball in a ledger entry about one of the tapes – it turns out to be the ball he was holding out to a dog at the very moment he realised that his mother had died: 'I shall feel it in my hand until my dying day,' his younger self says. His resolutions – to cut down on his drinking and his consumption of bananas – come to nothing. The play's final words (spoken by his younger self) that he wouldn't want his best years back, 'not with the fire in me now', are unspokenly contradicted by a decrepit Krapp whose fire has all but gone out and who clearly longs for past times. The most autobiographical words in the play, recalling Beckett's Sunday walks in the hills with his father, accompanied by the self-injunction 'Be again', will move some but strike others as oddly out of place in an otherwise near-perfect drama.

As much as the play reveals how self-serving and misleading memory can be, it also suggests that, for a writer at least, memory is key – and holds the key to whatever in life is worth preserving: precious little, in the Beckettian universe, but something all the same. (Perhaps, for the depressive personality subject to visionary moments, memory amounts to a kind of mysticism.) In the play, hopefulness is not wholly exposed as a hopeless lie. Even in this last tape, Krapp records that he 'Sometimes wondered in the night if a last effort mightn't –' before dismissing the half-hopeful thought with: 'Ah finish your booze now and get to your bed.'

As with *Molloy*, release follows the death of the mother. The blind goes down, signifying she has died, while he sits in the park holding a small black rubber ball: suddenly the ball is more physically real to him, and now motherless he might be said to have the whole world – a small rubber ball held out to a dog – in his hands.

While on a punt in the lake, Krapp also broke with the woman in his life: 'I said again I thought it was hopeless and no good going on.' This seems to him almost heroic at the time. It is as though he were fulfilling the poet Rilke's impossibly high-minded injunction to lovers to part so that they might experience their feelings more intensely in solitude:

> Is it not time that, in loving,
> we freed ourselves from the loved one, and, quivering, endured ... ?

Any exhilaration he might have felt following this loss has long since evaporated, and now only loss remains. What matters to the old man is not the younger man's resolution, but the girl with the scratch on her thigh from picking gooseberries.

Diary-like recall has become, with the interval of years, reminiscence. Krapp the failed writer voices some of the best passages ever written by Beckett: passages almost Keatsian in their lyricism. This is another aspect of the play's appeal. Ultimately, it is the 'human, all too human' nature of *Krapp's Last Tape* that has made it a hit with the public. Beckett usually preferred the extreme case, but remorseful types like Krapp can be found in any street, often very close to home.

Another play in English, *Embers* is essentially about the father and the feelings of inadequacy a son can experience at the hands of his father. As such, it both is and isn't personal: we know Beckett felt he had let his father down, notably by giving up his Trinity post; yet it presents a grotesque distortion of the warm relations between Bill and Sam. Beckett was always capable of such grotesquery – its presence in the more obviously autobiographical early work causing offence to some who were close to him. As warm as the Beckett father-son relationship undoubtedly was, it is quite conceivable that, in anger, Bill Beckett might have called his indolent son a 'washout', as Henry's father does when his son refuses to join him for a swim. Or perhaps Sam might have surmised this opinion from a look or a shrug. Distorting such hurt into grotesque fantasy may well be protective for the depressed self. For however bad things were, they were never really *this* bad, were they?

Embers is very precisely a play for radio. Beckett resisted attempts to stage it, apparently because this would make the character of Ada real when she may in fact only be the figment of Henry's imagination – an odd explanation by a writer who deals so adeptly with dramatising voices in the head.

In the play, the main (and arguably only) character, Henry, tells how he continues to live by the sea in which his father apparently drowned, perhaps intentionally; he finds the noise of the sea maddening, and tries to drown it out by speaking over it. At first, he told stories only; now he needs to hear the voices of lost ones and so be in their company again. He addresses his father repeatedly but hears no reply: 'I suppose you have worn him out,' explains the voice of his wife, Ada. Ada and Henry discuss their daughter Addie, whom Henry found insufferable – on walks she would interrupt his interior conversations – and who herself suffered at the hands of her music master and her riding instructor. Throughout, Henry returns to the story he is retelling, about a man called Bolton who has called out his doctor, Holloway, after midnight, to plead with him for some unspecified favour (a lethal injection, perhaps, or simply company).

Bolton stands in his dressing gown before a dying fire – the embers of the play's title. Just as blowing on embers causes them to glow while hastening their combustion, so Henry's plundering of memory for company is increasing his solitude, hastening the time when there will be nothing left but his own voice. Henry remembers, but less and less reliably or consolingly. (Is not the word 'embers' itself like the charred remains of 'remembers'?)

Some find this play not only unsettling but unsatisfying – Beckett himself conceded that it was 'ragged'. Did Henry's father commit suicide, or not? Does the Bolton-Holloway story refer to Henry or his father? It seems pointless to try to resolve its ambiguities.

Ada's voice recounts her visit to Henry's home when the family discovered that Henry's bed hadn't been slept in, causing his panicked sister to threaten to throw herself off a cliff. The suggestion of suicide spreads from Henry to his sister and then to his father.

The Bolton-Holloway story does come across as a fantasy of the father rather than a memory of the son: the setting and characters are reminiscent of an apparently solid bourgeois world, a solidity evoked in Larkin's poem 'Days', where the question 'Where can we live but days?' prompts the lines:

> Ah, solving that question
> Brings the priest and the doctor
> In their long coats
> Running over the fields.

Actually, this deceptively solid bourgeois world of frock-coated doctors was fatally exposed and undermined several decades earlier in the plays of the Russian physician, Anton Chekhov. Is Bolton-Holloway a kind of Beckettian-Chekhovian joke? As an exposé of the father, it is as reliable as Sylvia Plath's famous poem 'Daddy', in which her dead German father, a professor who wrote a book about bumblebees, is portrayed as a Nazi tyrant. A sick fantasy, perhaps, but really only a 'projection' in the way that all writing ultimately is, only palpably so.

One criticism of *Embers* voiced by John Pilling is that 'The failure to incorporate into the physical existence of the play its most important figure is not so much a failure of conception ... as of tact. There seems to be no good reason for the omission.' This might seem an odd accusation to level at an author whose most celebrated work is all about the omission of its most important character. It could also be argued that, in *Embers*, the father is in fact everywhere, from the overbearing sound of the sea to the naming of Henry's wife and daughter (Ada/Dad, Addie/Daddy). Yet Pilling's objection highlights an important facet of the play. One answer to it is that, however close a son and father might be or have been, a father cannot be a Muse to the son. It is right that the voice which Henry hears in his interior world is a woman's. Consider another play that is mainly about the father-son dynamic, Shakespeare's *Hamlet*, where the inward poetry of the play is embodied by the distraught Ophelia (and evident in the tender scene between Hamlet and his mother, Gertrude) while the play's male-centred action has a certain mechanicalness to it – from the father's ghost in clunking armour to the post-duel corpse-littered stage of the final act. *Embers* is hardly *Hamlet*, but it is an intriguing work by a writer whose 'use of poetic imagery', as John Calder observed, 'can be compared to Shakespeare's'.

Happy Days was the last Beckett play of any real length. Completed in 1961, it brings to the fore a feature of Beckett's plays – self-deceiving cheerfulness – which merely punctuated the gloom before. Estragon in *Godot* could appreciate the scenery, saying, 'Charming spot. Inspiring prospects,' immediately following this up with, 'Let's go.' Winnie, one half of the middle-aged couple that alone peoples *Happy Days*, sustains her cheerfulness despite being buried up to her waist (to her neck by the second act). Even as her 'dressed-to-kill' husband Willie crawls, possibly towards a 'conspicuous' revolver, she declares: 'Oh this is a happy day, this will have been another happy day!'

A full look at the worst (to use Thomas Hardy's phrase) can be liberating, but perpetual nay-saying is hard to stomach. *Happy Days* also says nay, but more cheerfully. Indeed, the critic Al Alvarez said of *Happy Days* that it is 'the most cheerful play Beckett has written and the least interesting'. One can see his point. Yet, with its mordantly bleak view of human existence everywhere evident, *Happy Days* is really no more cheering than any other Beckett work. Winnie's glass-full observations are so obviously wide of the mark that the play becomes too heavily reliant on irony. Despite the detachment and sometimes cruel comedy of much of Beckett's work, it remains affecting because we know that behind it all lies Beckett's own, unfaked despair. But in *Happy Days* the audience and author are placed in a position of superiority to Winnie. This is doubly galling since her manner of speaking is closer to the way ordinary people deal with the inevitable disappointments of their lives. Winnie's casual, 'Oh well, what does it matter?', is more the speech of ordinary mortals than is Pozzo's 'They give birth astride of a grave' from *Godot*. For all that, the sustained ironic cheerfulness of *Happy Days* brings some welcome variety to Beckett's *oeuvre*, even if it is only a slight variation on the usual theme.

Another variation is the play *Play*. Here we have a particular situation to explain the despair of the protagonists – if 'protagonists' is not too active a word for three figures encased in funeral urns, who speak only when 'provoked' by a spotlight shining on their faces. That situation is adultery, an eternal triangle whose eternity may well be Hell.

Play was written in 1962-63, shortly after Beckett married his long-time companion Suzanne Déchevaux-Dumesnil, ostensibly to secure inheritance rights for her, but also possibly as a declaration of intent to his 'mistress', the distinguished translator and BBC script editor Barbara Bray, who had announced that she was moving with her children to Paris to be near him. (Her relationship with him endured until Beckett's death.)

Yet despite the potential to mine his own personal circumstances for this play, Beckett chose to make the characters two-dimensional ciphers: the man M1, and the two women W1 and W2. Doubtless Beckett's sojourn in rural and seaside southern England – a legal requirement for marrying Suzanne there – exposed him to the genteel middle-class speech of the local inhabitants. Astonishingly, this monologic modernist play has many of the linguistic hallmarks of drawing-room comedy. That the stage directions require the lines to be delivered rapidly (even more rapidly in the second half) shows that Beckett wasn't showing off – the language isn't savouring itself, as it sometimes is in the drama of, say, Noel Coward or Oscar Wilde. This is classic Beckett tragi-comedy – a mordant humour in the face of despair.

The plot of the affair being continually retold by the characters is simple. W1 threatens suicide, accusing M1 of having an affair with a woman whose smell she detects on him; M1 denies this, and W1 has him followed by a private investigator, whom M1 bribes into reporting his innocence; just as she begins to believe in this, M1 (alarmed by the thought that she may actually kill herself) confesses all. W1 confronts W2, and the affair cools off for a while. Then M1 elopes with W2 before tiring of her also and leaving.

The three are left, as it were, in limbo (or their own private hells), both W1 and W2 imagining that M1 is with the other still, and M1 having fantasies of the three of them being together and getting along, boating and so on – rather as in the Thomas Hardy poem 'Over the Coffin' in which, at a man's graveside, his first wife tells the second wife:

> I would I had let alone you two!
> And both of us, scorning parochial ways,
> Had lived like the wives in the patriarchs' days.

At least Beckett places this sentiment in the mouth of the male character of *Play* – it belonging very clearly to the realm of male fantasy.

The musicality of *Play* – eg the three characters speaking simultaneously is referred to as a 'chorus', and there are references to 'tempo' in the stage directions – has been noted by several commentators. The whole play is repeated at the end, after a short reprise which acts as a kind of coda. Just how sure-footed a dramatic ploy this repetition is may be in some doubt, given the uncharacteristic vagueness of Beckett's instruction, 'The repeat may be an exact replica of first statement or it may present an element of variation' – though perhaps, given the oddness of the idea, this was merely a concession to directors. The clichéd, stilted Home Counties-style speech is brilliantly done, but it means that the specifically Beckettian music so rooted in his Irish upbringing (if tempered by his adoption of French) is lacking.

It wasn't long in returning. In 1965, after a brief foray into film with the speechless *Film*, and the sparse 'dramaticule' for the stage, *Come and Go*, Beckett began writing the powerful 'piece for television', *Eh, Joe*. Here we have a similar theme to that of *Embers*, with a man haunted by the most recent inner voice from his past – again, a woman's voice. But the treatment of that theme is more straightforward, less open to misunderstanding than in *Embers*. And the voice is more mind-hammeringly on the attack.

Joe is a man in his late 50s, moving about his room in dressing gown and slippers, childishly checking behind doors, out of the window and under the bed, before 'sitting on edge of bed, relaxed, eyes closed'. When the woman's voice 'starts in on' him, his eyes open and he listens intently. She is a former lover, whom he got rid of while telling her that the best was yet to come: a heartless act he repeated on another young woman – 'The green one ... The narrow one' – but more tragically, since she ended up taking her own life, an act described by the woman's voice with almost sexual relish (suggesting, of course, that the thought of the girl's suicide excites Joe himself). Before she gets to that, she upbraids him on other scores: that he might run out of loved ones' voices eventually; that there is no one living who loves him now, unless the attentions of the 'slut' who visits him weekly constitute love; that he has reduced her once-powerful voice to this colourless monotone bordering on a whisper; that he might one day, fatally, hear the voice of the God he foolishly believes in; that she had found another man who was 'preferable in all respects'.

The camera advances on Joe nine times, stopping each time the voice starts/resumes. The number, a magical one in many cultures, may or may not be significant here. One significant number in relation to this play is 59: Beckett began writing the piece on his 59th birthday. Might this have prompted a remorseful look back *a la* Krapp? *Eh, Joe* is one of the most convincing such texts in Beckett's oeuvre, looking forward to that masterly late prose work (also – partly – in the second person), *Company*.

Beckett had wanted his favoured actress, Billie Whitelaw, to perform the voice, but she was unavailable for the original TV production. Fortunately, she was available in 1989, the year of Beckett's death, for a production featuring Klaus Herm as Joe: this is easily found online.

The rapid-fire mouth of *Not I* is one of the most iconic images of Beckett's work. And yet there is a difficulty with it. As conceived by Beckett, *Not I* is a play for the theatre, but it is probably viewed by most on the screen – whether the BBC2 TV production with Billie Whitelaw, or Neil Jordan's version for the *Beckett on Film* series. The Beckett estate has been vigilant in preserving the author's production wishes and avoiding the kind of cross-over from one medium to another which distorts the original intentions of a piece. Yet Beckett himself approved the cross-over in this case.

Seeing, from some distance, a mouth lit up on stage is a very different experience from seeing a mouth close up on a TV or cinema screen. Also, in the theatre version, there is an additional character to Mouth – an 'Auditor' of indeterminable sex, wrapped in a black djellaba (a loose-hooded robe traditionally worn by Arabs), who makes brief movements of helpless compassion (a sideways raising of the arms) at four points in the monologue. In a production which he oversaw himself, Beckett found it too difficult to accommodate the Auditor and had this character removed – yet he couldn't bring himself to remove it from the published version of the play. Close up, the woman's mouth speaking rapidly may remind one of the 'vagina dentata' (toothed vagina) of folklore and Freud. But whichever production one sees, what will not be seen are the eyes – and it is the eyes one looks at most often when watching somebody speak, with occasional glances at the mouth and other features. Unsettlingly, *Not I* has no eyes in it.

The play runs for a few pages and lasts no longer than twenty minutes. It is a masterpiece of concision, yet the words seem to tumble from 'Mouth' as if unchecked. The premise is simple: a woman who has never been loved, even as a child, is mute for years until she experiences an uncontrolled talking fit, which recurs every so often, once being the 'action' of the play. She may have experienced a sudden trauma, but Beckett firmly rejected any speculation as to what this trauma might have been, telling the director Alan Schneider: 'All I know is in the text. "She" is purely a stage entity, part of a stage image and purveyor of a stage text.'

Not I is effectively *The Unnamable* in a nutshell. Here again we have personal identity breaking down, and in its place a mental and linguistic chaos. The woman cannot utter the word 'I', though she is aware of this and speaks in the third person about her failure to do so.

The play has both philosophical and psychological force. Philosophically, Beckett had come to believe that identity was an illusion, and that language itself was impossibly flawed. Joyce advised the young Beckett to read Fritz Mauthner, a relatively obscure philosopher of language who proposed that nothing was certain outside language, not even the existence of the self, and that laughter and silence were the highest forms of language critique (also, intriguingly, that communication between men is impossible – a point surely not missed on the future author of *Waiting for Godot*). 'There is no communication because there is no vehicle of communication,' wrote Beckett. This is a view that can be supported or opposed, unlike *Not I*, which is a work of art that either appeals or does not appeal but cannot be challenged – not even in terms of psychological accuracy, since 'she' is merely the 'purveyor of a stage text'.

Beckett said that he meant the play to work on the nerves rather than the intellect, and so it does. Still, if we slow the impact of the piece by reading rather than watching, we can isolate and pore over details that might otherwise be missed. As a small instance, take the moment of paralysis experienced by the woman one April morning, when 'wandering in a field ... looking aimlessly for cowslips ... to make a ball ... '. What does this refer to – making a ball with cowslips? Cowslip is a plant that produces yellow flowers in spring, and it was once a custom for children to make small yellow balls out of the flower heads and string, then toss the balls to one another while reciting the verse:

> Tissty-tossty, tell me true,
> Who am I going to be married to?
> Tinker, tailor, soldier, sailor,
> Rich man, poor man, beggarman, thief.

This has pathos in the context of an unloved woman. Cowslip balls were also thought to be useful in keeping away witches and the devil. The unloved girl has turned into something of a witch – a crone, at least. Remembering his childhood in Ireland, Beckett said of this character: 'There were so many of those old crones, stumbling down the lanes, in the ditches, besides the hedgerows.' The crone can be a powerful mythological figure – in Robert Graves's theory of the Muse as White Goddess, the crone is one of the female figures of the Triple Goddess (the others being maiden and mother). The banshee of Irish mythology, wailing near somebody who is about to die, appears both as an ugly crone and as a beautiful young woman. Beckett powerfully conflates withered age and imagery of spring here. The Latin name for cowslip, *primula veris*, means 'first of spring', while its English name is said to derive from the Old English for cow dung – almost a Beckettian irony in itself.

A study of intense isolation, *Not I* wasn't an isolated phenomenon in Beckett's oeuvre. A 'brother to *Not I*' was how Beckett characterised *That Time*. This short one-act play also contains a powerful visual image, of a smiling pasty-looking old man with 'long flaring white hair as if seen from above'. The smile, the meaning of which is unclear, comes only at the play's end. The play works less well than *Not I*. At this stage of his life and career, Beckett's dramatic imagination responded with greater pathos to the plight of the suffering woman.

This assertion is borne out by *Footfalls*, Beckett's next major short work for the stage – and his last. There would be other, increasingly diminutive (or decreasingly substantial) plays, notably *Ohio Impromptu*, which partially resembles an eviscerated *Krapp's Last Tape*. The lyricism of *Footfalls* also evokes some of the more poetic passages of *Krapp's Last Tape* – and like his majestic late prose work *Company*, both of these plays were written in English, confirming that Beckett eventually found a way of writing poetically but not over-poetically in his native tongue.

Footfalls is essentially a ghost story. Some commentators have pointed out the relevance of Jung's remark about a woman patient of his never having been born properly – a remark Beckett took to heart as an explanation of his own existential dread. Ghosthood implies an incomplete death rather than birth: the daughter of the play might be said never to have been born properly and the mother never to have died properly. The 'unborn' daughter is now ghostlike (by the play's end she is no longer there), while the (probably) dead mother lives on as a voice inside the daughter's head: as 'V' (for 'Voice'), the mother exists inside May, as the letter 'V' is found inside the letter 'M'.

The play is a striking mixture of the lyrical and the mathematical. May's sleepless pacing takes the form of nine steps along an illuminated strip from right to left before she 'wheels' and completes another nine steps from left to right, and so on: each length, Beckett insisted, should last exactly nine seconds. As the play progresses, the light fades and the bell sounds more quietly at the start of each scene, until eventually May is literally (as she has been psychologically) 'no longer there'. A miniature masterpiece, *Footfalls* is less an allegory of ageing than of death-in-life.

6

RUINS TRUE REFUGE

Fiction after the Trilogy

IN TERMS OF ATTRACTING CRITICAL ATTENTION, the thirteen untitled short pieces of *Texts for Nothing* have been notably unlucky. Beckett didn't help matters by describing them as *The Unnamable*'s 'grisly afterbirth'. They were originally published in French alongside *The Expelled*, *The Calmative* and *The End*, in a book entitled *Stories and Texts for Nothing* (Nouvelles et Textes pour Rien). A distinction is being made here between stories and non-stories. Just as Beckett had experienced a revelation in his mother's bedroom about the kind of writing he was to pursue, so too he appears in these pieces to be embodying the revelation that 'a story is not compulsory' and even that (in a rather un-Beckettian turn of phrase) 'life alone is enough'. So this bundle of non-stories is a significant development of Beckett's aesthetic of disintegration.

Commentators have pointed out the French title's allusion to a period of silence in music. Yet one element of the failure of these 'texts' to excite readers or critics is that, though they have the brevity of the later short fiction, they lack its 'music' (ie lyricism). The title in English evokes the expression 'thanks for nothing' – perhaps a more fitting allusion for a work that has an ungenerous, spiteful tone to it.

There is aggressive spite, too, in the voice that narrates the fragment *From an Abandoned Work*, which was written in English between 1954 and 1955. It may be that the return to English invigorated Beckett, for these few pages of negation possess vitality and even personality. What is related? Three days remembered by a 'mad' (or perhaps just 'a little strange') old man: in the first, he sets off early, with a backward look at his mother seemingly waving from the window, and later sees a white horse; in the second, out on a day-long walk, he ends up lying flat on the ground and being attacked by stoats; and in the third, he is disturbed by the leer of a roadman called Balfe who terrified him as a boy.

Of the roadman Balfe, the narrator says: 'Now he is dead and I resemble him.'

Balfe was the name of an actual roadman whom the young Beckett feared, but how autobiographical is the rest of this piece? There is the usual Beckettian horror of the mother, the long walks with the father (on one of these, explaining Milton's cosmology to him), and the dysfunctional adult hauntedly obsessed by those early relationships. The rage and lovelessness described might seem exaggerated in biographical terms, but Beckett allows such negative emotions to be expressed in their extreme, raw state, as they exist within the psyche before they are mediated by the demands of everyday life.

The story is what survives of an abandoned novel. It is like one of those short bursts of running which, the narrator says, allows him to 'vent the pent', ie discharge some of the energy behind his pent-up rage. It isn't difficult to see why it would have been a struggle for Beckett to have maintained this intensity over a longer work. And perhaps it's just as well that he didn't – *From an Abandoned Work* retains an energy undissipated by repetition.

Contrastingly, Beckett's final novel – if the word 'novel' can be applied to so unorthodox a literary work – harnesses the dissipating effects of repetition. Apostrophes aside, *How It Is* (Comment C'est) is wholly unpunctuated – emotional inflection is stripped from its succession of brief prose islands. Like Joyce's *Finnegans Wake*, it lies at the outer limits of comprehension, straining the reader's stamina almost to breaking point. Yet if you listen to an audio book of this work, with an actor bringing out the feelings behind the unpunctuated words, it really isn't so hard to follow. That said, the robotic voice of a 'text-to-speech' generated audio sounds truer to Beckett's intention here. *How It Is* isn't emotionless, but the emotion is buried deep.

The story, such as it is, describes the tormentor-victim relationship in three parts: before, during and after. The story's narrator is the tormentor, and his victim is Pim. The narrator anticipates being tormented in turn by a character he calls Bom – which is possibly his own name. Beckett summed up the novel thus:

> A 'man' is lying panting in the mud and dark murmuring his 'life' as he hears it obscurely uttered by a voice inside him ... The noise of his panting fills his ears and it is only when this abates that he can catch and murmur forth a fragment of what is being stated within.

A recurring mantra of this first-person narrative is 'before Pim with Pim after Pim'. Other repeated phrases include 'I say it as I hear it', 'end at last', 'something wrong there', 'without quaqua' – quaqua being, possibly, the voice of us all 'when the panting stops', not unlike the cawing sound of a crow. The repeated phrases act like musical hooks, and also suggest a mind gathering itself back together again, intent on not unravelling completely. The words are ostensibly murmured by a disintegrated character moving through mud: he has a sack with some tins of food and a tin-opener (referred to almost always simply as an 'opener' – the phrase 'I opener', a pun on eye-opener, occurs). He has used this tin-opener to stab Pim in the buttocks as a signal to speak.

The landscape of mud could be straight from Dante's fifth circle of hell, beside the muddy river Styx where the wrathful and sullen are located – anger and resentment being the key emotions of the tormentor-victim relationship. Now Beckett, as described by those who knew him, was both gracious and humane, so what drew him so strongly to this theme of pain inflicted by one human being on another? One answer could be depression, which Freud saw as anger turned inward – the inner voice of depression unleashing its fury sadistically on the self. More recently, the Jungian psychoanalyst Donald Kalsched has postulated a 'self-care system' in which children whose dependency needs have been unmet or who have suffered trauma are protected from experiencing their unbearable pain by a protector figure in the psyche which, in time, becomes a persecutor figure (since it prevents the child from developing new coping strategies and learning to grow emotionally). As Kalsched writes in *The Inner World of Trauma*:

> 'Never again,' says our tyrannical caretaker, 'will the traumatised personal spirit of this child suffer this badly! Never again will it be this helpless in the face of cruel reality ... before this happens I will disperse it into fragments [dissociation], or encapsulate it and soothe it with fantasy [schizoid withdrawal], or numb it with intoxicating substances [addiction], or persecute it to keep it from hoping for life in this world [depression].'

The reader or student may or may not find this helpful in

understanding Beckett, but it is easy to overlook the unusualness – or, rather, extremity – of Beckett's vision. There is, indeed, 'something wrong there'. Beckett was unhappy from early on. How it was for him shaped how it is for us to read him. Thus, people often clutch at the seemingly life-affirming nature of this vision when it is expressed as 'I can't go on, I'll go on' or 'Fail better', and close their eyes and ears to its life-denying aspect. As Kalsched observed: 'Paradoxically, in the name of survival, the archetypal self-care system says "NO!" to life.'

The repeated 'yes' at the end of Molly Bloom's soliloquy in Joyce's *Ulysses* is also often seen as life-affirming – yes to life and love, or else (and also) a climactic masturbatory cry. The repeated yes at the end of *How It Is* is an unambiguous dismissal of almost everything that has gone before – yes, this story has been 'all balls' all along. It is worth persevering with this difficult novel to reach its moving finale. The only thing that isn't denied at the end is the aloneness in the mud and the dark. That's 'life' – the rest is fiction.

There was never to be any work as large or ambitious as *How It Is* in Beckett's later career, but the move towards minimalism fitted this writer perhaps more than any other, and there was still a remarkable late withered-flowering to come.

The longest of the short pieces written in the 1960s and 1970s is the rather drearily arid *The Lost Ones* (Le Dépeupleur), in which two hundred people, 'each searching for its lost one', roam a cylindrical space. Aspects of *The Lost Ones* were reworked, or recycled, as *Ping* (Bing).

Beckett's talent and need to write may seem to have been fizzling out – an impression not dispelled by the publication of a fragment entitled *Imagination Dead Imagine* (Imagination morte imaginez) or of eight brief texts, all but one of them written in French, under the title *Fizzles* (Pour finir encore et autres foirades). Inbetween the two was the short text *Lessness* (Sans), made up of 60 sentences placed in a container and chosen randomly by Beckett – twice, since the story is 'told' in two halves, with the same sentences in a different order. If this is an experiment too far for some readers (the astute critic Martin Seymour-Smith remarked that there is no point in reading it), it is yet a hypnotically lyrical piece of writing – and the element of chance doesn't make the writing any less Beckettian, just as the singer-songwriter David Bowie's use of 'cut-ups' (sentences written then cut into sections and rearranged) doesn't render the resulting songs any less Bowie-like.

In *Fizzles*, published in 1976, there is a discernible shift in tone away from the angry frustration of *Texts for Nothing*. In retrospect, the opening fizzle, 'Horn Came Always', can be seen to prefigure the style of Paul Auster's spare metaphysical detective story *Ghosts* from *The New York Trilogy* – a novel in which each character's name is that of a colour (a device used in Quentin Tarantino's film of a few years later, *Reservoir Dogs*):

> Horn came always at night. I received him in the dark. I had come to bear everything bar being seen. In the beginning I would send him away after five or six minutes. Till he learnt to go of his own accord, once his time was up. He consulted his notes by the light of an electric torch. Then he switched it off and spoke in the dark. Light silence, dark speech.

The style isn't maintained, perhaps for the good reason that Beckett was by this time supremely uninterested in taking fiction in a viable new direction – a task for heirs of his such as Auster and the Irish novelist John Banville.

Beckett's claim to fame as a great prose writer encompasses two trilogies, the first published in the 1950s and the second in the

1980s. *Nohow On*, which appeared in 1989 (the year that Beckett died), may be less of a single piece than the Trilogy consisting of *Molloy, Malone Dies* and *The Unnamable*, but its constituent parts perfectly distil the essence of Beckett, whose philosophy of lessness is seen best in these late lyrical flowerings.

The first and last of the novellas were written in English, and the middle one in French. If a work of fiction may be said to have a personality, then *Company*'s is a split one. It begins in the third person ('A voice comes to one in the dark. Imagine.'), shifts to the second person ('Your mind never active at any time is now even less than ever so.'), and then flips between the two throughout. It is a quintessentially Beckettian situation of a body lying in the dark assailed by an accusatory voice and another voice of chilly detachment. The passages in which this voice directly addresses the body as 'you' read autobiographically; the third-person passages are more coldly analytical. One criticism of the autobiographical passages is their sentimentality – it has been said that Beckett could master ideas but not feelings. However, the separation of heart and mind in this work necessarily pushes each to an extreme. These were aspects of Beckett the man, and of the writer too – compare the intellectually acidic tone of his critical writings, such as his study of Proust, with the emotion-filled passages of *Company* or *Krapp's Last Tape.*

Some of the second-person passages seem more autobiographical than others. One such is told with slight variation by Beckett three times in his oeuvre: as a boy, he is walking hand-in-hand with his mother when he makes a remark about the sky which is met with a cutting retort from her. In *Company*, the boy is asking the mother if the sky is not more distant than it appears; when she gives no answer, he reframes the question, asking if the sky does not appear less distant than it really is. This is enough to make her shake off his hand and utter some words he will never forget, though we don't hear what they are. It is a far cry from the young boy discussing Milton's cosmology on walks in the hills with his father.

What was there in the young Beckett's reflections which so disturbed his mother? Perhaps he failed to pick up on her emotional cues, instead displaying a cleverness which grated on her nerves.

The most powerful passage in *Company*, and arguably in all of Beckett's writing, has no reliance on sentimental autobiographical detail. (Beckett allowed the passage to be published separately as 'Heard in the Dark 1', in the anthology *New Writing and Writers 17*.) This is the passage beginning: 'The last time you went out the snow lay on the ground.' It recounts a walk across a snowy pasture, and a look back at the 'great swerve' of the footprints in the snow, ending: 'Almost as if all at once the heart too heavy. In the end too heavy.'

In the biography of Beckett, *The Last Modernist*, the poet Anthony Cronin writes of *Company*:

> If you abstract these voices, what is left is a straightforward, almost sentimental evocation of childhood such as many authors could have written, though perhaps few so well.

One is tempted to add: 'Let them try'.

An old woman dressed in black is evoked in *Ill Seen Ill Said* (Mal vu mal dit), lyrically and tremblingly, as though she might (to quote Yeats) 'vanish on the instant if the mind but change its theme'. Once again, we see the influence of Dante's *The Divine Comedy*, not least in its Hell-Purgatory-Heaven structure: the location of the woman's 'abode' is within a 'zone of stones', which is within a wider zone called the 'pastures', beyond which is the 'unknown'/'haze'/'paradise'. The woman traverses the boundaries on her regular visits to a tombstone. ('To live this life is not as easy as to cross a field,' wrote Boris Pasternak in a poem from his novel *Dr Zhivago*; in Beckett, crossing a field can be as arduous as making the journey through life.) Twelve enigmatic figures surround her – onlookers at her life's end.

If there is a code that holds the secret to this almost numinous text, then it is one that Beckett seems not to have wanted the reader to break. John Calder, the publisher of Beckett's books in English, recalls Beckett being displeased when Calder managed to crack a part of the code by identifying the Virgin Mary as one of the novella's female archetypes. And while critics are right to warn against too autobiographical an interpretation of the work, with the old woman merely a depiction of May Beckett, there is certainly a sense in which Beckett is tentatively feeling his way to exploring the ageing mother-figure – the crone, in Robert Graves's notion of the Triple Goddess – almost reverentially, as if he were finally doing his mother justice. As Beckett's biographer James Knowlson recalled:

> In the final months of his life, Beckett's feelings of love for his mother and remorse at having, as he saw it, let her down so frequently, struck me as still intense, almost volcanic. It was virtually the only 'no go' area in our conversations.

Knowlson conjectures that Beckett may only have been able to go into this area in writing such as *Ill Seen Ill Said*, 'where the "dark lady" is endowed with a quiet dignity and a nobility that manages to survive imminent disintegration and decay.'

The twelve 'guardians' may be interpreted biblically as the twelve Apostles, but equally in this 'zone of stones' they may be seen in the light of the Zodiac. Robert Graves's White Goddess-inspired lines come to mind:

> So each new victim treads unfalteringly
> The never altered circuit of his fate,

Bringing twelve peers as witness
Both to his starry rise and starry fall.

Who is the occupant of the tomb that the old woman visits? A
dead husband, perhaps. Or perhaps her victim-son.

But beyond speculating as to a code or codes behind Beckett's
work, one must simply give oneself up to experiencing the revelatory
qualities of the words themselves. A strong advocate of Beckett's
late work, John Banville has admitted to having had to read *Ill
Seen Ill Said* many times before it 'opened like a flower' to him one
evening on a Dublin train.

Worstward Ho, the title of Beckett's last prose work of any
significant length (though still only a few thousand words) is a
double pun – on 'worst word' and on the title of two literary works
called *Westward Ho!* The better known of these is Charles Kingsley's
mid-19th century adventure novel which Beckett had known since
childhood; the other is a Jacobean satirical drama co-written by
John Webster – a poet and dramatist who was, as T.S. Eliot wrote,
'much possessed by death'. Beckett dispenses with the exclamation
mark of the title – this is language at the precipice of silence, not a
shouting out.

If *Company* risked sentimentality and *Ill Seen Ill Said* explored
a fraught emotional territory for Beckett, then *Worstward Ho* marks
a return to an almost hypnotic, cerebral style in which feelings can
only be inferred. An argument could be made that these late works
are, in fact, prose poetry – and in that light, *Worstward Ho*'s is a
heavily-accented poetry, often with two beats per 'line' (if the prose
is so rearranged) – for instance:

Whose words?
Ask in vain.
Or not in vain
If say no knowing.

No saying.

These short bursts can sometimes be heard to fall into that most traditional of English poetic rhythms, the iambic pentameter (we know from Beckett's notebooks that he had been rereading *King Lear* and noting instances of the play's use of the word 'worst'):

> Backs turned both bowed with equal plod they go.
> The child hand raised to reach the holding hand.
> Hold the old holding hand. Hold and be held.

What is this work *about*? It takes *The Unnamable*'s famous final words, 'I can't go on, I'll go on', to the next level of despairing endurance, but stripped of any 'I', as if it is language or existence itself which is persevering in the face of futility. The imperative is to 'fail better' – though it could also be to 'fail worse', a phrase which also recurs in the work (though is less often quoted, and never by politicians).

No urge to endure is evident in Beckett's final offerings, the short *Stirrings Still* and even shorter prose poem *What Is the Word*. Now the near-incoherent modernist distrust and dismantling of language reads like a very elderly man's aphasia and entirely understandable desire for 'Oh all to end'.

When the end did come for this writer born on Good Friday, it came on 22 December 1989. Three days later would have been too neat an ending.

ADDITIONAL RESOURCES

Online and Digital

There is a wealth of Beckett studies, articles and productions available online. Websites come and go, and links can become broken, but one resource which has so far stood the test of time is the scholarly *Journal of Beckett Studies* published online by Edinburgh University Press.

Beckett on Film. A DVD of 19 Beckett plays shaped for the screen by 19 directors, including such prominent figures as Anthony Minghella, David Mamet, Damien Hirst, Neil Jordan and Atom Egoyan.

Many of the *Beckett on Film* productions can be found online too. Other productions worth searching for include the BBC's *Eh Joe* (1966) and *Not I* (1977, performed by Billie Whitelaw).

Biographies

James Knowlson's biography is the authorised version – Knowlson was Beckett's friend, and had access to more material than his other biographers. The Irish poet Anthony Cronin's biography lacks some detail but is well written. Deirdre Bair was a pioneer of Beckett biography, but her version suffers not only from lack of detail but also occasional inaccuracy; Beckett called it 'the Bair fantasy'.

Bair, Deirdre, *Samuel Beckett: A Biography* (New York and London, 1978)

Cronin, Anthony, *Samuel Beckett: The Last Modernist* (London, 1996)

Knowlson, James, *Damned to Fame: The Life of Samuel Beckett* (London, 1996)

Beckett on Beckett

Letters

Beckett agreed to the publication only of those letters that were relevant to his work. Despite this caveat, the letters run to four volumes and around 3,000 pages. There are insights but little analysis from Beckett, who claimed to know as much about his work as a plumber knows about the history of hydraulics.

The Letters of Samuel Beckett: Volume 1, 1929-1940; Volume 2, 1941-1956; Volume 3, 1957-1965; Volume 4, 1966-1989 (Cambridge University Press)

Interviews

The subtitle of the Knowlsons' book says it all: 'Uncollected Interviews with Samuel Beckett and Memories of Those Who Knew Him'

Knowlson, James and Elizabeth (eds), *Beckett Remembering, Remembering Beckett* (London, 2006)

Critical Studies

Alvarez, A, *Samuel Beckett* (London, 1973)

Kenner, Hugh, *Samuel Beckett: A Critical Study* (London, 1961)

Ricks, Christopher, *Beckett's Dying Words: The Clarendon Lectures 1990* (Oxford, 1993)

Companions

Ackerley, CJ, and Gontarski, Stanley, *The Faber Companion to Samuel Beckett: A Reader's Guide to His Life, Works, and Thought* (London, 2006)

Van Hulle, Dirk, *The New Cambridge Companion to Samuel Beckett* (Cambridge, 2015)